Pisces

1999

by the same author

TERI KING'S COMPLETE GUIDE
TO YOUR STARS

TERI KING'S ASTROLOGICAL HOROSCOPES
FOR 1999:

Aries 21 March to 20 April
Taurus 21 April to 21 May
Gemini 22 May to 21 June
Cancer 22 June to 23 July
Leo 24 July to 23 August
Virgo 24 August to 23 September
Libra 24 September to 23 October
Scorpio 24 October to 22 November
Sagittarius 23 November to 21 December
Capricorn 22 December to 20 January
Aquarius 21 January to 19 February

Pisces

Teri King's complete horoscope
for all those whose birthdays
fall between
20 February and 20 March

E L E M E N T

Shaftesbury, Dorset ● Boston, Massachusetts
Melbourne, Victoria

© Element Books Limited 1998
Text © Teri King 1998

First published in Great Britain in 1998 by
Element Books Limited
Shaftesbury, Dorset SP7 8BP

Published in the USA in 1998 by
Element Books, Inc.
160 North Washington St, Boston, MA 02114

Published in Australia in 1998 by
Element Books
and distributed by Penguin Books Australia Ltd
487 Maroondah Highway, Ringwood, Victoria 3134

Cover design by Max Fairbrother
Text design by Roger Lightfoot
Typeset by Palimpsest Book Production Limited
Polmont, Stirlingshire
Printed and bound in Great Britain by
Caledonian International Book Manufacturing, Glasgow

British Library Cataloguing in Publication
data available

Library of Congress Cataloging in Publication
data available

ISBN 1-86204-274-8

Element Books regrets that it cannot enter into any
correspondence with readers requesting information
about their horoscopes.

Contents

Introduction   1
The Sun in Pisces   5
A Fresh Look at Your Sun Sign   7
The Year Ahead: Overview   16
Career Year   19
Money Year   22
Love and Sex Year   24
Health and Diet Year   27
Numerology Year   29
Your Sun Sign Partner   52
Monthly and Daily Guides   63

Pisces

20th February – 20th March

Ruling Planet: Neptune
Element: Water
Quality: Feminine
Planetary Principle: Sacrifice
Primal Desire: Unification
Colour: Heliotrope
Jewel: Crysolite
Day: Thursday
Magical Number: 11

Famous Pisces

Elizabeth Taylor, Rudolph Nureyev, Frédéric Chopin,
Georg Friedrich Handel, Elizabeth Barrett Browning,
Michelangelo, Vaslav Nijinsky, Rembrandt,
George Harrison.

Introduction

Astrology has many uses, not least of these its ability to help us to understand both ourselves and other people. Unfortunately there are many misconceptions and confusions associated with it, such as that old chestnut – how can a zodiac forecast be accurate for all the millions of people born under one particular sign?

The answer to this is that all horoscopes published in newspapers, books and magazines are, of necessity, of a general nature. Unless an astrologer can work from the date, time and place of your birth, the reading given will only be true for the typical member of your sign.

For instance, let's take a person born on 9 August. This person is principally a subject of Leo, simply because the Sun occupied that section of the heavens known as Leo during 24 July to 23 August. However, when delving into astrology at its most serious, there are other influences which need to be taken into consideration – for example, the Moon. This planet enters a fresh sign every 48 hours. On the birth date in question it may have been in, say, Virgo. And if this were the case it would make our particular subject Leo (Sun representing willpower) and Virgo (Moon representing instincts) or if you will a Leo/Virgo. Then again the rising sign or 'ascendant' must also be taken into consideration. This also changes constantly as the Earth revolves: approximately every two hours a new section of the heavens comes into view – a new sign passes over the horizon. The rising sign is of the utmost importance, determining the image projected by the subject to the outside world – in effect, the personality.

The time of birth is essential when compiling a birth chart. Let us suppose that in this particular instance Leo was rising at the time of birth. Now, because two of the three main influences are Leo, our sample case would be fairly typical of his or her sign, possessing all the faults and attributes associated with it. However, if the Moon and ascendant had been in Virgo then, whilst our subject would certainly display some of the Leo attributes or faults, it is more than likely that for the most part he or she would feel and behave more like a Virgoan.

As if life weren't complicated enough, this procedure must be carried through to take into account all the remaining planets. The position and signs of Mercury, Venus, Mars, Jupiter, Saturn, Uranus, Neptune and Pluto must all be discovered, plus the aspect formed from one planet to another. The calculation and interpretation of these movements by an astrologer will then produce an individual birth chart.

Because the heavens are constantly changing, people with identical charts are a very rare occurrence. Although it is not inconceivable that it could happen, this would mean that the two subjects were born not only on the same date and at the same time, but also in the same place. Should such an incident occur, then the deciding factors as to how these individuals would differ in their approach to life, love, career, financial prospects and so on would be due to environmental and parental influence.

Returning to our hypothetical Leo: our example with the rising Sun in Leo and Moon in Virgo, may find it useful not only to read up on his or her Sun sign (Leo) but also to read the section dealing with Virgo (the Moon). Nevertheless, this does not invalidate Sun sign astrology. This is because of the great power the Sun possesses, and on any chart this planet plays an important role.

Belief in astrology does not necessarily mean believing in totally determined lives – that we are predestined and have no control over our fate. What it does clearly show is that our lives run in cycles, for both good and bad and, with the aid of astrology, we can make the most of, or minimize, certain patterns and tendencies. How this is done is entirely up to the individual. For example, if you are in possession of the knowledge that you are about to experience a lucky few days or weeks, then you can make the most of them by pushing ahead with plans. You can also be better prepared for illness, misfortune, romantic upset and every adversity.

Astrology should be used as it was originally intended – as a guide, especially to character. In this direction it is invaluable and it can help us in all aspects of friendship, work and romance. It makes it easier for us to see ourselves as we really are and, what's more, as others see us. We can recognize both our own weaknesses and strengths and those of others. It can give us both outer confidence and inner peace.

In the following pages you will find: personality profiles, an in-depth look at the year ahead from all possible angles including numerology; monthly and daily guides; your Sun sign partner; plus, and it is a big plus, information for those poor and confused creatures so often ignored who are born on 'the cusp' – at the beginning or the end of each sign.

Used wisely, astrology can help you through life. It is not intended to encourage complacency, since, in the final analysis, what you do with your life is up to you. This book will aid you in adopting the correct attitude to the year ahead and thus maximize your chances of success. Positive thinking is encouraged because this helps us to attract positive situations. Allow astrology to walk hand in hand with you and you will be increasing your chances of success and happiness.

The Sun In Pisces

You are vulnerable, softly spoken and sensitive. You choke up when reading tales of valour, sniffle at weddings and overwhelmed with remorse when it is time to end a relationship. Your innermost secret is your need to be cherished and nurtured. Even if, to compensate your feelings of vulnerability, you behave like Attila the Hun. Conversely, if you are worshipped, you still have a tendency to feel unloved in small ways and often force your lover to prove their feelings. In doing so, you sometimes bring a situation of pleasure far closer to one of pain.

The problem is you keep waiting for the prince/princess, except that your usual modern version is likely to be a playboy/playgirl. Unfortunately, you often pick the wrong people, although they seem good at the time. However, five years later when you start to feel like a martyr it might be a good idea for you to reconsider your choices. To you it seems that everyone else in the world is at some kind of glamorous ball, while all you do is stand in front of the mirror and look at your enlarged pores. If, as time goes by, you never find answers, only perhaps a few spots, then you know your life is in for some heavy changes.

Strangely enough, it's not easy for you to accept the love you need because it's far easier for you to be lonely than it is for you to believe you deserve some unsolicited attention. Needless to say, your self-image is not only hazy but hazardous. Although you're devoted to the act of self-improvement, you're the last one to see where and how you have improved. Because of this you are insecure and supersensitive to the feelings of your friends, and the saviour of crumpled souls and an inspirational force for those unfortunates who feel forsaken. Despite what you may at times feel, you are not at all weak. You are deeply feeling and afraid of showing your emotions. The experience of personal sorrow has brought you to a place of deep compassion and universal understanding. Essentially, you have the soul of an artist and your vision is one that could resurrect the consciousness of the world.

A Fresh Look at Your Sun Sign

As a rule, members of the general public appreciate and understand that for practical reasons Sun sign astrology is fairly general, and therefore for a more in-depth study it is necessary to hire an astrologer who will then proceed to study the date, year, place and time of birth of an individual. Then, by correlating the birth chart with the positions of the different planets, a picture can be drawn up for the client.

However, there is also a middle way, which can be illuminating. Each sign comprises 30 'degrees' (or days) and, by reducing these down into three sections, it becomes possible to draw up a picture of each sign which is far more intimate than the usual methods. Therefore, check out your date of birth and draw your own conclusions from the information below.

PISCES (20 February to 20 March)

BORN BETWEEN 20 FEBRUARY AND 1 MARCH

Your Sun falls in the first section of Pisces. Because of this you are a stereotype romantic who enjoys attempting to turn life into poetry in motion. You dwell on plans, dreams, self-induced drama and schemes. You are highly emotional, sentimental, wistful and occasionally melancholic. Certainly, you are artistic and creative and invariably overactive. Doggedly, you look for fantasies come true, divine highs and stimulating romantic situations. Furthermore, when confused you need solitude in order to sort out your more troubled feelings.

Generally speaking, the situations or reasons that induce your temporary gloom seem elusive and hazy, and quite often so is your state of mind. The emotional confusion frequently results in reclusive tendencies, and there are even days when you just cannot be bothered to stir yourself and get out of bed – usually because you simply don't want to. You then allow yourself to drift into a nostalgic or maudlin mood, and this is a temptation you should consciously strive to avoid. Once this mood strikes, you attempt to create an insulating cocoon around yourself in which you can ruminate, withdraw and analyse your emotions. However, despite this need to allow passiveness to take over, you usually have more internal resources at your fingertips than most people. Fundamentally, the problem is that often you simply don't know how to utilize them and they are left untended or ignored.

There is a strong likelihood that you possess psychic ability, an inventive and original mind and tremendous creative talent, all of which could flourish in occult study.

Basically, the problem you wrestle with is that your emotions often cripple you to the point where you are too afraid to carry out your own deep desires. It is necessary to think positively and make strenuous efforts to rise above the inclination to put yourself down and hold yourself back. When you have accomplished this you will find that it is far easier to make life a pleasure rather than a problem. But before this can be achieved you must decide that you are more interested in having a go at life than in giving up and passively allowing yourself to be consumed by dissatisfying situations.

BORN BETWEEN 2 MARCH AND 11 MARCH

Your Sun falls in the second section of Pisces. This means that you are more changeable, emotionally sensitive and impressionable than Pisces subjects born in the other sections. Furthermore, you are also more considerate, caring and imaginative. Despite a clear inclination to be idealistic, you also have within your power the means for making your dreams materialize. You are intelligent, intuitive and tenacious, and struggle to overcome negative emotional moods.

Nevertheless, mood swings and changes can undermine your self-confidence and feelings of self-worth, and because of this you should fight hard towards greater emotional balance and self-discipline. Deep within the reaches of your soul is a conflict between your attempts to make your practical ideas materialize and an inclination towards inaction.

Although you have a completely original mind, your dreamy-eyed moods can sometimes prevent progress and keep your plans in a state of dormancy. You possess a tremendous sense of timing but your inclination to wait things out frequently restricts and retards the ultimate results.

As a rule you have a deep enjoyment of life's more

sensual pleasures, plus an optimistic approach to life. When driven to extremity, your sybaritic sensibilities usually result in more trouble than you care to consider. It is therefore important that you learn to balance pragmatism with your impressionability or you are likely to become a victim of your own desires.

Once you have managed to discover the middle way between cool, lucid logic and heated inspiration, you will have the golden key to success at your disposal.

BORN BETWEEN 12 MARCH AND 20 MARCH

Your Sun falls in the third section of Pisces. This is an extremely powerful section of your sign because it is associated with change and rebirth. More than likely you carry around with you a heavy karma from which you need to free yourself through the use of spiritual forces. There is an inclination for you to allow painful memories to pull you back into the past. Nevertheless, it is imperative that you re-experience these memories just long enough to resolve them and then free yourself of them for ever.

Luckily, you are aware of the fact that new cycles of experience lie ahead. But before you can live life to the fullest extent, you must eliminate the dross which permeates your head and your life. This section is usually deeply aware of change at its most profound – on either a physical or psychological level. There is a strong possibility that you have undergone many serious changes in life, and such upheavals may have appeared more often than you could comfortably cope with. Nevertheless, on each occasion you have overcome your pain through the power within you.

It is likely that you will experience a great deal before you are ready to progress in life. Some of these experiences will be difficult to handle because invariably they will bring about some kind of loss. However, once you have pushed yourself into understanding the higher levels of consciousness you will be able to feel instinctively that what you are losing is only a negative experience or situation that threatens to imprison you unless you can eliminate it from your life.

Should you attempt to resist the natural changes in your life and prefer instead to cling to past memories, relationships and habits that only hamper your ability to grow, you will be creating unnecessary trouble for yourself. You must accept that at some point in life all such experiences will evaporate, whether you like it or not. Provided you are able to use each experience positively, firstly by becoming more self-aware and, secondly, by recognizing your spirituality, you will be moving towards the cycle of freedom illustrated in your following sign, Aries. The sign of the Ram represents new beginnings created by self-directed willpower: an unchained will that is free to make the changes that are necessary in order to realize one's full potential.

Crucial to this section is the idea of sacrifice. It is therefore important that you willingly sacrifice your old, negative life patterns before new, constructive ones can form. Should you be unwilling to do this, you will be allowing past experiences to pull you down.

You have the capability to develop a tremendous amount of psychic power and if you are willing to

do so you can grasp the highest power it is possible
to possess.

WHEN YOU ARE BAD YOU ARE VERY VERY BAD (Horrorscopes)

You seem to be addicted to stress, a person who rarely
tires of dramatizing life. Friends become exhausted
with the constant repetition of your difficulties. And
despite your repeated mistakes you never seem to learn
from them. You have an aggressive/passive character
that expresses anger in the most complicated way:
hysteria, hypochondria, sulking and sarcasm all are
utilized; despite the fact that they rarely get you
anywhere.

There is an inclination to hole up in a corner and, like
a hurt animal, lick your wounds in the hope that others
are watching. But since this is hardly the most effective
method of getting attention, you invariably end up sitting
by yourself feeling abandoned and neglected.

You often allow yourself to become consumed by
situations and people that have a negative effect on you
and drown in self-created unhappiness. It is on these
occasions that you roll over, weep your heart out and
play the loser.

For reasons that others find difficult to understand,
you find a certain sensationalism in sadness. You allow
yourself to be overcome by sentimentality and are easily
moved by melancholia. It is hardly surprising that your
idea of love is nothing short of a grand finale that

comes complete with enchantment: a package deal, if you like.

Because of your emotional immaturity, you frequently become involved with the wrong people. Your partners are often married, irresponsible and incapable of commitment. However, for reasons that only you understand, you are able to convince yourself that you can rehabilitate these hopeless cases. Subconsciously, these problem people help you to keep your distance and aid you in avoiding too much intimate contact. Regardless of this, you are not fazed: you are able to take on whatever you want and rarely listen to anybody, anyway. The fantasy side to your character is so ingrained that often you don't really need a mate – a mental trip is quite satisfactory. Your involvement with reality is so remote that it is an easy matter for you to avoid confronting anything you don't wish to. However, once you isolate yourself from what is going on in your life, you start to feel alienated, lonely and depressed.

Conversely, you are possessive about such mood swings, morose moments and depressions. You think you need solitude, not helpful advice. And even if you were given any it is unlikely that you would listen or show any gratitude. You prefer to hide rather than confront the world, just like a coward. Basically, you have little idea of what you really want, although you certainly make a fuss when you can't have it. Unless you face up to your own passiveness and stop complaining and analysing yourself, you will never be free from a permanent anxiety attack.

You may even prefer to live your life as a victim. If you do, then bear in mind that you really are your own worst enemy – no one in your life could possibly play the role as well as you do.

CUSP CASES

PISCES/AQUARIUS CUSP: 17–22 FEBRUARY

You may possibly be aware that this is one of the most talented cusps in the zodiac. This is because you are given the creative artistry of Pisces, plus the vision of Aquarius – a fascinating blend of objectivity and sensitivity. There is a strong possibility that you will be highly original, possibly psychic, and adventurous. When Neptune and Uranus are combined in this way you can accomplish the majority of your ambitions and objectives.

Your creativity is likely to incline you to music, poetry or the artistic world. You may have several marriages or long relationships before you are able to find that special someone who is able to understand you both emotionally and mentally.

PISCES/ARIES CUSP: 18–23 MARCH

This cusp contains an interesting blend of the driving, aggressive force of Mars and the inventive visions of Neptune. Because of this you will never be content to simply dream your life away. The Aries side of your character fills you with determination and will certainly boost your Piscean confidence. On the other hand, your Piscean sympathies and consideration will temper the Aries ego.

There is a strong possibility that you are a charming

individual with a theatrical inclination, blending positive and negative in a way which is hard for other people to pin down. You can be energetic, mystical and easy-going, and are, in truth, everybody's ideal mate.

The Year Ahead: Overview

The strength of your sign lies in ideals and aspirations, rather than action. You usually have little wordly ambition, care nothing for rank or power, seldom succeed in making money and rarely save it. You're indifferent about restrictions and limitations, so long as the inner self is left free to feel, dream and grow according to its own nature. Many Pisceans are attracted to the cloister or shrink from society and from any competition, rivalry and strife. Some go to sea, or spend available recreation time on an off-shore fishing boat, preferring the silent world of water. With the deep ocean below and the star-spangled sky above, you rest content, calm and fearless, because solitude and solitary thinking are frequently the luxuries most prized by you, especially if your life is in uncongenial surroundings.

It is difficult to say, however, that any particular profession is impossible or unsuitable for a Fish. Individual commercial enterprise is possible if the business signs – Taurus and Virgo – are accentuated on an individual's chart. But as a rule financial success is rarely the first consideration, it is instead fulfilment, satisfaction and necessity which drive a Fish on. So, what can a kind and gentle sign expect for the new year? Well, at the very least hope but only if you remember not to be fatalistic about astrology, simply identify the trends, work with them and then you will be making the most of the year ahead.

Pluto this year will be coasting along in the fiery sign of Sagittarius. This is the zenith point of your chart and the area of your profession, your reputation and perhaps the more powerful parent in your life, as well as other significant authority figures. This represents the challenge for you to become your own parent and authority figure. There's a strong chance this year therefore that, although you may be doing very well, you must take nothing for granted otherwise sudden beginnings and endings could throw you when you should look upon them as a challenge and a chance to learn.

Uranus and Neptune breeze their way through the air sign of Aquarius. For you, this sign represents self-imposed limitations, regrets, secrets, large institutions and possibly experiences involving mysticism, spiritualism, karma and possibly from a past life. This part of the chart for you completes the circle of experience and requires self-evaluation in respect of past relationships. You will need to make some serious readjustment of your values as well as your behaviour. It's quite likely then that you'll take the helm of your life for a change and make the necessary alterations that you feel have perhaps been holding you back.

Saturn will be coasting along in the area of your chart connected with money, possessions, wealth and values. You'll be given the chance to build on a lifetime of experience and appreciate your own self-worth. It's true you may have to work harder for your cash, but if you're prepared to do the necessary slog, then by the end of this year your finances are likely to rest on far more solid foundations than they have for some time.

Jupiter in Aries will be broadening your views and increasing a compulsion to show the world that you really count, which of course you do. You'll be feeling more optimistic and ready to grasp any opportunities which crop up to increase your happiness, as well as your bank account. From a materialistic and spiritual point of view, you will regard 1999 as an extremely important and lucky year.

Career Year

In general, your sign prefers a quiet life to one of competition. You look upon the anxiety ridden super-achievers with a certain disdain. Therefore, if you are what is referred to as a typical Piscean, it is likely that you desire to be a comfortable bystander rather than a highly stressed mogul. Your mind seeks a haven from the nagging worries of the outside world, so the pandemonium of a business office would not only exhaust but depress you. You are the artist, the poet, the psychic, the mystic and the musician. Because of your vital imagination and need to escape the hectic world, acting and writing can provide a creative outlet for you. Painting, sculpting and film-making are also fruitful areas where you could succeed.

Although there may be changes, some of them enforced where work matters are concerned, the placing of Jupiter in your sign means that whatever occurs will work out well in the end. All you need to do is have faith, which is something a Piscean usually has in abundance, though it weakens occasionally in the face of life's blows. Luckily you seem to be protected by Jupiter's lucky rays, so there's nothing for you to worry about there.

During January, you may be filled with enthusiasm

but must remember that this is the month for making plans for the rest of the year. From 18 February through to 20 March you're given extra determination to push for what you need to enhance your reputation and career. This is a particularly good month for those who are freelance workers and many of you will be signing important documents, or perhaps travelling for the sake of business.

From 20 March through to 20 April it's an especially lucky time for the Fish who is involved with the monied professions, or for those who want to put something away for the proverbial rainy day. Yes, just for once, you'll be saving and feeling quite virtuous.

From 21 April through to 20 May it is the Piscean involved in sales, the media or short-distance travelling who will do well. Furthermore, if you happen to be out of work, this is the time to act because you could be lucky. From 21 May through to 22 June it is the Fish who is professionally involved in property and its allied trades who will be doing exceptionally, and also for those who are thinking of moving house.

From 23 June through to 22 July the Fish who is professionally involved with children, all kinds of creativity or sports should have precious little to complain about, though you may be able to find something if you try. From 23 July through to 23 August, unless you are off on your holidays, and this might be a good idea, it's going to be a hard-working period and one when you'll have your nose to the grindstone and you may not feel the benefits immediately.

From 24 August through to 22 September you are advised to cooperate with other people as much as

possible. If the chance arises for you to join forces
with somebody else, may I suggest that you snap it up
because this could be extremely lucky for you. Besides,
it's always useful to have somebody else around to help
make those very difficult decisions, isn't it?

From 23 September through to 23 October your own
work seems to be pretty routine but you may be concerned with those you might be financially dependent
upon, so be 'there' for them when the need arises. From
24 October through to 22 November the Fish who is
employed in higher education or long-distance travelling
and foreign affairs in general should be enjoying a
profitable time. You'll be reaching out into life in a
big way and your new-found sense of adventure will
certainly be paying off.

From 23 November through to 21 December, regardless of your job, you'll be working hard, keeping a high
profile and this will eventually bring you in the rewards
you so richly deserve.

Money Year

Money slips through your fingers like quicksilver and you quite clearly have no idea why. You especially love to spend it on dreary days when you feel lost and abandoned in the doldrums. Luxury gives you pleasure and some champagne can easily help you through the night – along with silk sheets and, an elegant body to keep you company. However you don't require a country estate with a team of servants (although it would be nice), but you do crave comfort and sometimes your vision of it can be quite costly. So how are you going to fare during the year ahead?

The year may get off to a difficult start because there's a strong possibility, where finance is concerned, that bureaucrats and officials may be giving you a hard time, but as long as you have been straightforward in all of your dealings you'll have nothing to worry about. February finds you swelling your coffers through foreigners, long-distance travel and matters related to abroad, so wherever you hear a strange sounding accent prick up those ears.

March will be difficult due to Mars' retrograde action, so it's rather a time when you may be finding it difficult to move forward, though it's unlikely that you'll move backwards. This trend continues throughout April through to June when Mars finally resumes direct movement on the 4th.

During July, your affairs seem to be very much tied up with other people, but the hints, tips and advice they are giving you are good and sound and so, perhaps, you should listen to them. This inclination continues throughout August and it is only on 3 September through to 16 October that you are able to free yourself and be your own person where cash is concerned. If you are asked to work any kind of overtime, you should seriously consider it because it will bring added security.

From 17 October through to 25 November you will gain through teamwork and advice handed on to you through friends or acquaintances. From 27 November through to the remainder of the year you should use your instincts and intuition when handling financial matters, because then you'll be put on the right track.

Love and Sex Year

Although you often loathe your vulnerable side, you're a wild romantic itching for emotional intensity. You want your soul to be swept away by nothing less than a grand passion. You're a highly charged sensualist who would love to live out your fantasies. However, in such situations you often let your emotions get the better of you. You're an emotionally attached lover living in a dream of how exquisite life could be if only . . . However, when you feel like a bitter, jaded, loveless victim, remember that it was you who made all the choices and compromised a sense of total satisfaction in order to gain emotional security that exists only in your mind's eye. But what about the year ahead?

Well, you need to watch out between 5th and 29th January because somehow you could be attracted to people who are simply not good for you. They may be married or possibly not telling you the truth about something. From 29 January through to 21 February Venus will be in your sign and so you are provided with the chance of meeting many new people and possibly that special someone too. If you're already in a relationship, you may consider becoming engaged or married and you couldn't have picked a better time for doing just that.

From 23 February through to 17 March you are more materialistic than is usually the case. If you have two admirers, well, then the one who is the most comfortably off from a financial viewpoint is the one who will be attracting your attention. From 18 March through to 12 April you're in a casual mood, preferring to take your admiration as well as attention wherever you can get it, rather than seriously considering entering into a lifelong commitment.

From 13 April through to 8 May you're appreciating your loved ones and your family and really couldn't care less if the love of your life decides to remain elusive. From 9 May through to 5 June you're once more in a casual mood, but you're certainly not going to be short of admirers and can afford to be as picky and as choosy as you want.

From 6 June through to 12 July it's likely to be your work that will bring opportunities for you to meet the opposite sex, though you are still reluctant to commit yourself to any one person. From 13 July through to 7 October it is workmates and work itself which will provide you with opportunities for meeting the opposite sex, but there will be complications at various points during this period and you need to refer to the *Monthly and Daily Guides* to find out when.

From 8 October through to 9 November there is a rosy glow over all of your relationships. If you are fancy-free, then you could meet someone really special, whilst other Fish will be ready to make some kind of commitment. During December Venus will be in the watery sign of Scorpio, suggesting a strong attraction with people from foreign lands, or those who have something 'different' about them. You're not interested in just a run-of-the-mill romance simply for the sake of it.

Now for further information refer to the *Monthly and Daily Guides*.

Health and Diet Year

Your sign rules over phosphate of iron, commonly known as ferrum phosphoricum. This cell salt has a great affinity for oxygen and is the means by which oxygen enters the bloodstream. Foods that are particularly useful to you are plants and vegetables, preferably grown organically because any iron elements come from the soil and carry them to the leaves where they form chlorophyll, the green colouring matter of nature. You should ensure that your diet includes a percentage of foods containing iron. These foods are of greater value if eaten raw as cooking tends to destroy the iron content unless they are carefully cooked.

Foods that are good for you are dried peas, beans, green leafy vegetables, such as spinach and lettuce, dried fruits, such as raisins, dates, figs and prunes, nuts, cereals, root vegetables and all fresh fruit. If you can eat at least one of these foods daily, then you should remain in disgustingly good health and perhaps in contradiction to your belief because, let's face it, there are times when you can be something of a hypochondriac. But how healthy will you stay during 1999?

During January, you'll be working extremely hard and must set aside some time for real relaxation when you can let the whole world drift away, even if it means hiring a load of romantic videos just to keep you in one place.

From February through to 6 July don't allow the financial affairs of other people to drag you down. From 6 July through to 2 September you only need worry if you are travelling abroad, in which case may I suggest that you get your shots well in advance and be a little bit more picky when eating foreign foods.

From 3 September through to 17 October your only difficulty could come from exhaustion due to hard work, so slow yourself down and take things a little easier during this time. From 17 October through to 27 November you may be a little clumsy which could lead to minor mishaps, but apart from this you should stay healthy. From 28 November for the remainder of the year that brain of yours will be travelling at the speed of light, so once again clumsiness could be a slight problem.

Now for further information please turn to the *Monthly and Daily Guides.*

Numerology Year

In order to discover the number of any year you are interested in, your 'individual year number', first take your birth date, day and month, and add this to the year you are interested in, be it in the past or in the future. As an example, say you were born on 9 August 1995:

$$
\begin{array}{r}
9 \\
8 \\
1995 \\
\hline
2012 \\
\hline
\end{array}
$$

Then, write down $2 + 0 + 1 + 2$ and you will discover this equals 5. This means that the number of your year is 5. If the number adds up to more than 9, add these two digits together.

You can experiment with this method by taking any year from your past and following this guide to find whether or not numerology works out for you.

The guide is perennial and applicable to all Sun signs: you can look up years for your friends as well as for yourself. Use it to discover general trends ahead, the way you should be approaching a chosen period and how you can make the most of the future.

INDIVIDUAL YEAR NUMBER 1

GENERAL FEEL

A time for being more self-sufficient and one when you should be ready to grasp the nettle. All opportunities must be snapped up, after careful consideration. Also an excellent time for laying down the foundations for future success in all areas.

DEFINITION

Because this is the number 1 individual year, you will have the chance to start again in many areas of life. The emphasis will be upon the new; there will be fresh faces in your life, more opportunities and perhaps even new experiences. If you were born on either the 1st, 19th or 28th and were born under the sign of Aries or Leo then this will be an extremely important time. It is crucial during this cycle that you be prepared to go it alone, push back horizons and generally open up your mind. Time also for playing the leader or pioneer wherever necessary. If you have a hobby which you wish to turn into a business, or maybe you simply wish to introduce other people to your ideas and plans, then do so whilst experiencing this individual cycle. A great period too for laying down the plans for long-term future gains. Therefore, make sure you do your homework well and you will reap the rewards at a later date.

RELATIONSHIPS

This is an ideal period for forming new bonds, perhaps business relationships, new friends and new loves too. You will be attracted to those in high positions and with strong personalities. There may also be an emphasis on bonding with people a good deal younger than yourself. If you are already in a long-standing relationship, then it is time to clear away the dead wood between you which may have been causing misunderstandings and unhappiness. Whether in love or business, you will find those who are born under the sign of Aries, Leo or Aquarius far more common in your life, also those born on the following dates: 1st, 4th, 9th, 10th, 13th, 18th, 19th, 22nd and 28th. The most important months for this individual year, when you are likely to meet up with those who have a strong influence on you, are January, May, July and October.

CAREER

It is likely that you have been wanting to break free and to explore fresh horizons in your job or in your career and this is definitely a year for doing so. Because you are in a fighting mood, and because your decision-making qualities as well as your leadership qualities are foremost, it will be an easy matter for you to find assistance as well as to impress other people. Major professional changes are likely and you will also feel more independent within your existing job. Should you want times for making important career moves, then choose Mondays or Tuesdays. These are good days for pushing your luck and presenting your ideas well. Changes connected with your career are going to be more likely during April, May, July and September.

HEALTH

If you have forgotten the name of your doctor or dentist, then this is the year for going for check-ups. A time too when people of a certain age are likely to start wearing glasses. The emphasis seems to be on the eyes. Start a good health regime. This will help you cope with any adverse events that almost assuredly lie ahead. The important months for your own health as well as for loved ones are March, May and August.

INDIVIDUAL YEAR NUMBER 2

GENERAL FEEL
You will find it far easier to relate to other people.

DEFINITION
What you will need during this cycle is diplomacy, co-operation and the ability to put yourself in someone else's shoes. Whatever you began last year will now begin to show signs of progress. However, don't expect miracles; changes are going to be slow rather than at the speed of light. Changes will be taking place all around you. It is possible too that you will be considering moving from one area to another, maybe even to another country. There is a lively feel about domesticity and in relationships with the opposite sex too. This is going to be a marvellous year for making things come true and asking for favours. However, on no account should you force yourself and your opinions on other people. A spoonful of honey is going to get you a good deal further than a spoonful of vinegar. If you are born under the sign of Cancer or Taurus, or if your birthday falls on the 2nd, 11th, 20th or 29th, then this year is going to be full of major events.

RELATIONSHIPS

You need to associate with other people far more than is usually the case – perhaps out of necessity. The emphasis is on love, friendship and professional partnerships. The opposite sex will be much more prepared to get involved in your life than is normally the case. This is a year your chances of becoming engaged or married are increased and there is likely to be an increase in your family in the form of a lovely addition and also in the families of your friends and those closest to you. The instinctive and caring side to your personality is going to be strong and very obvious. You will quickly discover that you will be particularly touchy and sensitive to things that other people say. Further, you will find those born under the sign of Cancer, Taurus and Libra entering your life far more than is usually the case. This also applies to those who are born on the 2nd, 6th, 7th, 11th, 15th, 20th, 24th, 25th or 29th of the month.

Romantic and family events are likely to be emphasized during April, June and September.

CAREER

There is a strong theme of change here, but there is no point in having a panic attack about that because, after all, life is about change. However, in this particular individual year any transformation or upheaval is likely to be of an internal nature, such as at your place of work, rather than external. You may find your company is moving from one area to another, or perhaps there are changes between departments. Quite obviously, then, the most important thing for you to do in order to make your life easy is to be adaptable. There is a strong possibility too that you may be given added responsibility. Do not flinch as this will bring in extra reward.

If you are thinking of searching for employment this year, then try to arrange all meetings and negotiations on Monday and Friday. These are good days for asking for favours or rises too. The best months are March, April, June, August, and December. All these are important times for change.

HEALTH

This individual cycle emphasizes stomach problems. The important thing for you is to eat sensibly, rather than go on, for example, a crash diet – this could be detrimental. If you are female then you would be wise to have a check-up at least once during the year ahead just to be sure you can continue to enjoy good health. All should be discriminating when dining out. Check cutlery, and take care if food has only been partially cooked. Furthermore, emotional stress could get you down, but only if you allow it. Provided you set aside some periods of relaxation in each day when you can close your eyes and let everything drift away, then you will have little to worry about. When it comes to diet, be sure that the emphasis is on nutrition, rather than fighting the flab. Perhaps it would be a good idea to become less weight conscious during this period and let your body find its natural ideal weight on its own. The months of February, April, July and November may show health changes in some way. Common sense is your best guide during this year.

INDIVIDUAL YEAR NUMBER 3

GENERAL FEEL

You are going to be at your most creative and imaginative during this time. There is a theme of expansion and growth and you will want to polish up your self-image in order to make the 'big impression'.

DEFINITION

It is a good year for reaching out, for expansion. Social and artistic developments should be interesting as well as profitable and this will help to promote happiness. There will be a strong urge in you to improve yourself; either your image or your reputation or perhaps your mind. Your popularity soars through the ceiling and this delights you. Involving yourself with something creative brings increased success plus a good deal of satisfaction. However, it is imperative that you keep yourself in a positive mood. This will attract attention and appreciation of all of your talents. Projects which were begun two years ago are likely to be bearing fruit this year. If you are born under the sign of Pisces or Sagittarius, or your birthday falls on the 3rd, 12th, 21st or 30th, then this year is going to be particularly special and successful.

RELATIONSHIPS

There is a happy-go-lucky feel about all your relationships and you are in a flirty, fancy-free mood. Heaven help any-one trying to catch you during the next twelve months: they will need to get their skates on. Relationships are likely to be light-hearted and fun rather than heavy going. It is possible too that you will find yourself with those who are younger than you, particularly those born under the signs of Pisces and Sagittarius, and those whose birth dates add up to 3, 6 or 9. Your individual cycle shows important months for relationships are March, May, August and December.

CAREER

As I discussed earlier, this individual number is one that suggests branching out and personal growth, so be ready to take on anything new. Not surprisingly, your career aspects look bright and shiny. You are definitely going to be more ambitious and must keep up that positive façade and attract opportunities. Avoid taking obligations too lightly; it is important that you adopt a conscientious approach to all your responsibilities. You may take on a fresh course of learning or look for a new job, and the important days for doing so would be on Thursday and Friday: these are definitely your best days. This is particularly true in the months of February, March, May, July and November: expect expansion in your life and take a chance during these times.

HEALTH

Because you are likely to be out and about painting the town all the colours of the rainbow, it is likely that health problems could come through over-indulgence or perhaps tiredness. However, if you have got to have some health problems, I suppose these are the best ones to experience, because they are under your control. There is also a possibility that you may get a little fraught over work, which may result in some emotional scenes. However, you are sensible enough to realize they should not be taken too seriously.

If you are prone to skin allergies, then these too could be giving you problems during this particular year. The best advice you can follow is not to go to extremes that will affect your body or your mind. It is all very well to have fun, but after a while too much of it not only affects your health but also the degree of enjoyment you experience. Take extra care between January and March, and June and October, especially where these are winter months for you.

INDIVIDUAL YEAR NUMBER 4

GENERAL FEEL

It is back to basics this year. Do not build on shaky foundations. Get yourself organized and be prepared to work a little harder than you usually do and you will come through without any great difficulty.

DEFINITION

It is imperative this year that you have a grand plan. Do not simply rush off without considering the consequences and avoid dabbling of any kind. It is likely, too, that you will be gathering more responsibility and on occasions this could lead you to feeling unappreciated, claustrophobic and perhaps over-burdened in some ways. Although it is true to say that this cycle in your individual life tends to bring about a certain amount of limitation, whether this be on the personal side to life, the psychological or the financial, you now have the chance to get yourself together and to build on more solid foundations. Security is definitely your key word at this time. When it comes to any project, or job or plan, it is important that you ask the right questions. In other words, do your homework before you go off half-cock. That would be a disaster. If you are an Aquarius, a Leo or a Gemini or you are born on the 4th, 13th, 22nd, or the 31st of any month, this individual year will be extremely important and long remembered.

RELATIONSHIPS

You will find that it is the eccentric, the unusual, the unconventional and the downright odd that will be drawn into your life during this particular cycle. It is also strongly possible that people you have not met for some time may be re-entering your circle and an older person or somebody outside your own social or perhaps religious background will be drawn to you too. When it comes to the romantic side of life, again you are drawn to that which is different from usual. You may even form a relationship with someone who comes from a totally different background, perhaps from far away. Something unusual about them stimulates and excites you. Gemini, Leo and Aquarius are your likely favourites, as well as anyone whose birth number adds up to 1, 4, 5, or 7. Certainly, the most exciting months for romance are going to be February, April, July and November. Make sure then that you socialize a lot during this particular time, and be ready for literally anything.

CAREER

Once more we have the theme of the unusual and different in this area of life. You may be plodding along in the same old rut when suddenly lightning strikes and you find yourself besieged by offers from other people and, in a panic, not quite sure what to do. There may be a period when nothing particular seems to be going on, when to your astonishment you are given a promotion or some exciting challenge. Literally anything can happen in this particular cycle of your life. The individual year 4 also inclines towards added responsibilities and it is important that you do not offload them onto other people or cringe in fear. They will eventually pay off and in the meantime you will be gaining in experience and paving the way for greater success in the future. When you want to arrange any kind of meeting, negotiation or perhaps ask for a favour at work, then try to do so on a Monday or a Wednesday for the luckiest results. January, February, April, October and November are certainly the months when you must play the opportunist and be ready to say yes to anything that comes your way.

HEALTH

The biggest problems that you will have to face this year are caused by stress, so it is important that you attend to your diet and take life as philosophically as possible, as well as being ready to adapt to changing conditions. You are likely to find that people you thought you knew well are acting out of character and this throws you off balance. Take care, too, when visiting the doctor. Remember that you are dealing with a human being and that doctors, like the rest of us, can make mistakes. Unless you are 100 per cent satisfied then go for a second opinion over anything important. Try to be sceptical about yourself because you are going to be a good deal more moody than usual. The times that need special attention are February, May, September and November. If any of these months fall in the winter part of your year, then wrap up well and dose up on vitamin C.

INDIVIDUAL YEAR NUMBER 5

GENERAL FEEL

There will be many more opportunities for you to get out and about and travel is certainly going to be playing a large part in your year. Change too must be expected and even embraced – after all, it is part of life. You will have more free time and choices, so all in all things look promising.

DEFINITION

It is possible that you tried previously to get something off the launching pad, but for one reason or another it simply didn't happen. Luckily, you now get a chance to renew those old plans and put them into action. You are certainly going to feel that things are changing for the better in all areas. You are going to be more actively involved with the public and will enjoy a certain amount of attention and publicity. You may have failed in the past but this year mistakes will be easier to accept and learn from; you are going to find yourself both physically and mentally more in tune with your environment and with those you care about than ever before. If you are a Gemini or a Virgo or are born on the 5th, 14th or 23rd then this is going to be a period of major importance for you and you must be ready to take advantage of this.

RELATIONSHIPS

Lucky you! Your sexual magnetism goes through the ceiling and you will be involved in many relationships during the year ahead. You have that extra charisma about you which will be attracting others and you can look forward to being choosy. There will be an inclination to be drawn to those who are considerably younger than yourself. It is likely too that you will find that those born under the signs of Taurus, Gemini, Virgo and Libra as well as those whose birth date adds up to 2, 5 or 6 will play an important part in your year. The months for attracting others in a big way are January, March, June, October and December.

CAREER

This is considered by all numerologists as being one of the best numbers for self-improvement in all areas, but particularly on the professional front. It will be relatively easy for you to sell your ideas and yourself, as well as to push your skills and expertise under the noses of other people. They will certainly sit up and take notice. Clearly, then, a time for you to view the world as your oyster and to get out there and grab your piece of the action. You have increased confidence and should be able to get exactly what you want. Friday and Wednesday are perhaps the best days if looking for a job or going to negotiations or interviews, or in fact for generally pushing yourself into the limelight. Watch out for March, May, September, October or December. Something of great importance could pop up at this time. There will certainly be a chance for advancement; whether you take it or not is, of course, entirely up to you.

HEALTH

Getting a good night's rest could be your problem during the year ahead, since that mind of yours is positively buzzing and won't let you rest. Try turning your brain off at bedtime, otherwise you will finish up irritable and exhausted. Try to take things a step at a time without rushing around. Meditation may help you to relax and do more for your physical wellbeing than anything else. Because this is an extremely active year, you will need to do some careful planning so that you can cope with ease rather than rushing around like a demented mayfly. Furthermore, try to avoid going over the top with alcohol, food, sex, gambling or anything which could be described as 'get rich quick'. During January, April, August, and October, watch yourself a bit, you could do with some coddling, particularly if these happen to be winter months for you.

INDIVIDUAL YEAR NUMBER 6

GENERAL FEEL

There is likely to be increased responsibility and activity within your domestic life. There will be many occasions when you will be helping loved ones and your sense of duty is going to be strong.

DEFINITION

Activities for the most part are likely to be centred around property, family, loved ones, romance and your home.

Your artistic appreciation will be good and you will be drawn to anything that is colourful and beautiful, and possessions that have a strong appeal to your eye or even your ear. Where domesticity is concerned, there is a strong suggestion that you may move out of one home into another. This is an excellent time too for self-education, for branching out, for graduating, for taking on some extra courses – whether simply to improve your appearance or to improve your mind. When it comes to your social life you are inundated with chances to attend events. You are going to be a real social butterfly, flitting from scene to scene and enjoying yourself thoroughly. Try to accept nine out of ten invitations that come your way because they bring with them chances of advancement. If you are born on the 6th, 15th or 24th or should your birth sign be Taurus, Libra or Cancer then this is going to be a year that will be long remembered as a very positive one.

RELATIONSHIPS

When it comes to love, sex and romance the individual year 6 is perhaps the most successful. It is a time for being swept off your feet, for becoming engaged or even getting married. On the more negative side, perhaps there is a separation and divorce. However, the latter can be avoided, provided you are prepared to sit down and communicate properly. There is an emphasis too on pregnancy and birth, or changes in existing relationships. Circumstances will be sweeping you along. If you are born under the sign of Taurus, Cancer or Libra, then it is even more likely that this will be a major year for you, as well as for those born on dates adding up to 6, 3 or 2. The most memorable months of your year are going to be February, May, September and November. Grab all opportunities to enjoy yourself and improve your relationships during these periods.

CAREER

A good year for this side to life too, with the chances of promotion and recognition for past efforts all coming your way. You will be able to improve your position in life even though it is likely that recently you have been disappointed. On the cash front, big rewards will come flooding in mainly because you are prepared to fulfil your obligations and commitments without complaint or protest. Other people will appreciate all the efforts you have put in, so plod along and you will find your efforts will not have been in vain. Perversely, if you are looking for a job or setting up an interview, negotiation or a meeting, or simply want to advertise your talents in some way, then your best days for doing so are Monday, Thursday and Friday. Long-term opportunities are very strong during the months of February, April, August, September and November. These are the key periods for pushing yourself up the ladder of success.

HEALTH

If you are to experience any problems of a physical nature during this year, then they could be tied up with the throat, nose or the tonsils plus the upper parts of the body. Basically, what you need to stay healthy during this year is plenty of sunlight, moderate exercise, fresh air and changes of scene. Escape to the coast if this is at all possible. The months for being particularly watchful are March, July, September and December. Think twice before doing anything during these times and there is no reason why you shouldn't stay hale and hearty for the whole year.

INDIVIDUAL YEAR NUMBER 7

GENERAL FEEL

A year for inner growth and for finding out what really makes your tick and what you need to make you happy. Self-awareness and discovery are all emphasized during the individual year 7.

DEFINITION

You will be provided with the opportunity to place as much emphasis as possible on your personal life and your own wellbeing. There will be many occasions when you will find yourself analysing your past motives and actions, and giving more attention to your own personal needs, goals and desires. There will also be many occasions when you will want to escape any kind of confusion, muddle or noise; time spent alone will not be wasted. This will give you the chance to meditate and also to examine exactly where you have come to so far, and where you want to go in the future. It is important you make up your mind what you want out of this particular year because once you have done so you will attain those ambitions. Failure to do this could mean you end up chasing your own tail and that is a pure waste of time and energy. You will also discover that secrets about yourself, and other people could be surfacing during this year. If you are born under the sign of Pisces or Cancer, or on the 7th, 16th or 25th of the month, then this year will be especially wonderful.

RELATIONSHIPS

It has to be said from the word go that this is not the best year for romantic interest. A strong need for contemplation will mean spending time on your own. Any romance that does develop this year may not live up to your expectations but, providing you are prepared to take things as they come without jumping to conclusions, then you will enjoy yourself without getting hurt. Decide exactly what it is you have in mind and then go for it. Romantic interests this year are likely to be with people who are born on dates that add up to 2, 4 or 7 or with people born under the sign of Cancer or Pisces. Watch for romantic opportunities during January, April, August and October.

CAREER

When we pass through this particular individual cycle, two things in life tend to occur: retirement from the limelight, and a general slowing down, perhaps by taking leave of absence or maybe retraining in some way. It is likely too that you will become more aware of your own occupational expertise and skills – you will begin to understand your true purpose in life and will feel much more enlightened. Long-sought-after goals begin to come to life if you have been drifting of late. The best attitude to have throughout this year is an exploratory one when it comes to your work. If you want to set up negotiations, interviews or meetings, arrange them for Monday or Friday. In fact, any favours you seek should be tackled on these days. January, March, July, August, October and December are particularly good for self-advancement.

HEALTH

Since, in comparison to previous years, this is a rather quiet time, health problems are likely to be minor. Some will possibly come through irritation or worry and the best thing to do is to attempt to remain meditative and calm. This state of mind will bring positive results. Failure to do so may create unnecessary problems by allowing your imagination to run completely out of control. You need time this year to restore, recuperate and contemplate. Any health changes that do occur are likely to happen in February, June, August and November.

INDIVIDUAL YEAR NUMBER 8

GENERAL FEEL

This is going to be a time for success, for making important moves and changes, a time when you may gain power and certainly one when your talents are going to be recognized.

DEFINITION

This individual year gives you the chance to 'think big'; it is a time when you can occupy the limelight and wield power. If you were born on the 8th, 17th or 26th of the month or come under the sign of Capricorn, pay attention to this year and make sure you make the most of it. You should develop greater maturity and discover a true feeling of faith and destiny, both in yourself and in events that occur. This part of the cycle is connected with career, ambition and money, but debts from the past will have to be repaid. For example, an old responsibility or debt that you may have avoided in past years may reappear to haunt you. However, whatever you do with these twelve months, aim high – think big, think success and above all be positive.

RELATIONSHIPS

This particular individual year is one which is strongly connected with birth, divorce and marriage – most of the landmarks we experience in life, in fact. Lovewise, those who are more experienced or older than you, or people of power, authority, influence or wealth will be very attractive. This year will be putting you back in touch with those from your past – old friends, comrades, associates, and even romances from long ago crop up once more. You should not experience any great problems romantically this year, especially if you are dealing with Capricorns or Librans, or with those whose date of birth adds up to 8, 6 or 3. The best months for romance to develop are likely to be March, July, September and December.

CAREER

The number 8 year is generally believed to be the best one when it comes to bringing in cash. It is also good for asking for a rise or achieving promotion or authority over other people. This is your year for basking in the limelight of success, the result perhaps of your past efforts. Now you will be rewarded. Financial success is all but guaranteed, provided you keep faith with your ambitions and your-self. It is important that you set major goals for yourself and work slowly towards them. You will be surprised how easily they are fulfilled. Conversely, if you are looking for work, then do set up interviews, negotiations and meetings, preferably on Saturday, Thursday or Friday, which are your luckiest days. Also watch out for chances to do yourself a bit of good during February, June, July, September and November.

HEALTH

You can avoid most health problems, particularly headaches, constipation or liver problems, by avoiding depression and feelings of loneliness. It is important when these descend that you keep yourself busy enough not to dwell on them. When it comes to receiving attention from the medical profession you would be well advised to get a second opinion. Eat wisely, try to keep a positive and enthusiastic outlook on life and all will be well. Periods which need special care are January, May, July and October. Therefore, if these months fall during the winter part of your year, wrap up well and dose yourself with vitamins.

INDIVIDUAL YEAR NUMBER 9

GENERAL FEEL

A time for tying up loose ends. Wishes are likely to be fulfilled and matters brought to swift conclusions. Inspiration runs amok. Much travel is likely.

DEFINITION

The number 9 individual year is perhaps the most successful of all. It tends to represent the completion of matters and affairs, whether in work, business, or personal affairs. Your ability to let go of habits, people and negative circumstances or situations, that may have been holding you back, is strong. The sympathetic and humane side to your character also surfaces and you learn to give more freely of yourself without expecting anything in return. Any good deeds that you do will certainly be well rewarded, in terms of satisfaction and perhaps financially too. If you are born under the sign of Aries or Scorpio, or on the 9th, 18th or 27th of the month, this is certainly going to be an all-important year.

RELATIONSHIPS

The individual year 9 is a cycle which gives appeal as well as influence. Because of this, you will be getting emotionally tied up with members of the opposite sex who may be outside your usual cultural or ethnic group. The reason for this is that this particular number relates to humanity and, of course, this tends to quash ignorance, pride and bigotry. You also discover that Aries, Leo and Scorpio people are going to be much more evident in your domestic affairs, as well as those whose birth dates add up to 9, 3 or 1. The important months for relationships are February, June, August and November. These will be extremely hectic and eventful from a romantic view-point and there are times when you could be swept off your feet.

CAREER

This is a year which will help to make many of your dreams and ambitions come true. Furthermore, it is an excellent time for success if you are involved in marketing your skills, talents and expertise more widely. You may be thinking of expanding abroad for example and, if so, this is certainly a good idea. You will find that harmony and cooperation with your fellow workers are easier than before and this will help your dreams and ambitions. The best days for you if you want to line up meetings or negotiations are going to be Tuesday and Thursday and this also applies if you are looking for employment or want a special day for doing something of an ambitious nature. Employment or business changes could also feature during January, May, June, August and October.

HEALTH

The only physical problems you may have during this particular year will be because of accidents, so be careful. Try too to avoid unnecessary tension and arguments with other people. Take extra care when you are on the roads: no drinking and driving for example. You will only have problems if you play your own worst enemy. Be extra careful when in the kitchen or bathroom: sharp instruments that you find in these areas can lead to cuts, unless you take care.

Your Sun Sign Partner

PISCES WITH PISCES

This relationship starts off as sheer poetry. However, after they return to earth, what's next? Someone's going to have to pitch in with some realism, but the chances are that neither of them really knows where to begin. They both smile, look searchingly at the other and mutter 'well . . .' As time passes they could lead each other to the heights or to an indefinite stay in the depths. It all depends where they prefer to spend their time and money.

Pisces woman with Aries man

For her it's almost love at first sight, whether or not she wants to show it, but that's just for sexual starters. After the first few nights he's still in the running for total ravagement of your mind and body. However, after she witnesses how selfish he can be in the daytime, with the sun shining in his eyes, then it's quite another matter if the love continues.

She is still searching for the knight on a white charger to come and whisk her away. Superficially, he'll fulfill her fantasies, but underneath not only will he not understand her, he won't even have the patience to try.

Pisces woman with Taurus man

He is like a big castle that she can lean up against, and only a Taurus man could stand the weight. She is fragile, a vulnerable creature with a mental make-up that he'll never understand. He is the solid force with a matter-of-fact philosophy that totally mystifies her because it's so simple.

The compatibility here is not exactly brilliant, however, the underlying needs that are satisfied are something else. They both tend to be enslaved by the sensual pleasures that quicken the pulse and speed up the bloodstream. They both like to sleep in the sun and sip cold drinks to the strains of a love song. They both could adore a marathon of sex from dawn till dusk, and prefer a body that is naked to one that is nicely dressed. Together, they could become a worthwhile team, if their divergent approaches to life don't get in the way.

Pisces woman with Gemini man

They are both mysteries, but the difference is that she has depth. She is emotional, sympathetic, compassionate and moody. He is cerebral, self-centred, critical and moody. Despite the externals, deep down she is shy and unsure of herself. More often than not, she will find him uncaring and he'll find her confining. Deep down inside she wants emotional security, while he seeks the perfect state of freedom. He can be callous and abrupt with her. Her feelings are badly bruised when he conspicuously ignores her at a dinner party. But her feelings fly away when later he whispers a clever love line in her ear. In between the heights of misery he'll make her feel that life's not worth living. It isn't, not with him.

Pisces woman with Cancer man

The psychic rapport of this match will leave her starry eyed. He will sympathize with her mood swings, cry along with her at a movie and remember what she wore on the day he first met her. She will marvel that he is a better cook than she is. He is sensitive and seems to know not only what she is thinking, but why. Prepare for a lifetime of love on the beach, under the stars or beside a bowl of roses and an open window that lets the moonlight peep in.

Pisces woman with Leo man

She'll whine around a lot, which can be pretty boring, but what she does in bed is something else altogether. She is a super-sensualist. She talks through her body and her language leaves him speechless. Naturally, he'll like to have her around, but being the restless sort it's a question of how long. For a while they will feed each others dreams and the air will wreak with romance. In this relationship neither of them cherishes the light of day. It's candle light and love all the way to the wedding. But loneliness may result if they emerge from the mental mist unprepared.

Pisces woman with Virgo man

She finds comfort in chaos, while he craves the kind of order found from control. She longs for a life of never-ending emotional excitement. He prefers the kind of stability that could give her sleeping sickness. She is emotionally moved by movies, glamorous nights on the town and ghost stories. He is moved by the mechanics of his mind and the number of shelves in his filing cabinet. He doesn't value poetry because it can't be proven. She, on the other hand, can't see the importance of his structures because they leave no room for spontaneity. Their differences are entirely too great for a happy relationship. Her sensitivities are desperate enough for the kind of divorce that seems to deny there was ever any love at all.

Pisces woman with Libra man

He will probably never understand her moods, chaotic emotions or for her need for far more reassurance than he wants to give. She is fearful of her feelings, while he has a way of enjoying his. He relies on reasoning to gather insights. She knows that her intuition would get her anywhere. He sees the world as a fascinating puzzle, while she feels it in pastel shades. Sexually, she will sweep him off his feet, but emotionally he may feel that she brings him down. Unless he has a very high sense of awareness, this relationship is not an equal one.

Pisces woman with Scorpio man

Sexually, this combination is so powerful that they may both end up on the floor. She'll control him through her desire, and he'll devour her through his control. They may both expire because of the sheer exhaustion of the situation, but what a lovely way to go. Since this kind of chemistry is narcotic they should be prepared to get hooked. It may come to the point where they stop eating, sleeping and thinking and start losing weight. Any way you look at it, this is a 'sex is all' kind of love story. Indoors there are no limits, but what to do when it's snowing and they are standing in silence on the street. The chances are he'll do something to make her start crying so that he can take a deep breath and walk away.

Pisces woman with Sagittarius man

She'll fall in love with his boyish charm and wild enthusiasm. But after a while she will realize that his warmth can be turned on quite casually and impersonally at will. He'll be seduced by her steamy sensuality and will delight in her daily do-good attitude. He is friendly and very charming, but when it comes to women he's like a used-car salesman who lives in anticipation of next year's model. If you can view this encounter as a brief but fantastic affair rather than a future marriage prospect, then nothing will be lost.

Pisces woman with Capricorn man

He'll be the father figure she's searched for and she'll be the woman of romance. She needs a strong man she can rely on, and he needs a woman who knows how to need. She'll boost his ego when she comes running to him for his advice and a shoulder to cry on. In turn, he'll tell her what to do and demand that she follows his instructions implicitly. He provides her with some practicality, while she provides him with a poetic sensitivity that he never knew he had. Together, if they are determined to learn from their differences, they can create a love relationship that will put them in touch with themselves as well as each other.

Pisces woman with Aquarius man

Although she respects his intelligence, it wears her nerves

a little thin when it's midnight and he's still babbling on about his latest electronic microscope.

He has absolutely no idea where she's coming from, but he has a wealth of theories. However, each of them, while truly interesting, somehow misses the mark by a long shot. He filters the world through his mind, while she sifts it through her emotions.

As a serious love affair this probably won't be long-lasting. Both of them are lovable people, but the emotional differences will eventually drive them apart.

Pisces man with Aries woman

Her temper will give him nightmares, but what she does to his daydreams is quite another matter. He is destined to fall flat on his face in love, but she won't want to hear about it. He's too subjective for her sensitivities and has a way of making her feel like she's working in a clinic for the emotionally disturbed. He tries her patience, never gets to the point and drives her to a state of insanity with his moods. He will see her as a sadomasochistic kind of challenge. She sees him as a noose around her neck that keeps getting tighter. At the end, through his tears, he'll wish her the worst. But she'll be so happy that she'll wish him the best as she burrows her way out of his life forever.

Pisces man with Taurus woman

He is a fantasy addict, while she prefers facing the facts. If she marries him, she'll take on the responsibility of a caretaker in a home for the insane. He can't be bothered with day-to-day details, so she has to assume what he shuns. He is overflowing with sympathy for the underprivileged, however, should she develop an acute case of pneumonia, he'll still expect her to take the car for the yearly checkup. In the divorce court, he'll tell his solicitor that she taught him a lot. What he taught her is that marriage is not really the wonder she hoped it might be.

Pisces man with Gemini woman

This combination is so incongruous that the only qualities they have in common are that they are both human (hopefully) and alive (even more hopefully). In a short period of time she will mutter to herself that he is just awash with emotions. At the same time, he will think quite secretly that she is nothing but a chatterbox and an emotional void. What he won't admit is that even if he can't stand her, she's also such a challenge that he feels he loves her. After a while, she will just wish he'd go off and drown himself in his emotions. However, he still daydreams that her glacial heart will give him a chance, but the only chance she's willing to consider is a peaceful parting.

Pisces man with Cancer woman

He'll find her so nice to cuddle with. She will provide many seductive creature comforts and the emotional back up that he needs to do his best. Not only is she warm and sensitive, she has the kind of womanly strength that reminds him of mother. She will understand his moods, listen to his problems and give a lot of loving assistance for those projects he knows he'll never finish. In essence, this combination could be a divine exploration into the deepest experience of loving. The communication here can carry them to the farthest plains of feeling.

Pisces man with Leo woman

He will fall in love fast and send her up into the sky with verbal splendour. Unfortunately, he goes on talking too long.

The younger she is, the better this partnership. If she's had a few Pisceans in her lifetime, she is probably wary and impatient. She'll tell him that she has time to listen for only a brief while.

At 60 he will still seek a romance more fabulous than his fantasies. Needless to say, he rarely finds it, but he will never stop looking.

Although he means well, he is held back by a withered super-ego. In his fantasy world of ideals, guilt has no place. He is capable of being honest about many things, but not about himself. He embraces the infantile idea of romance and dwells on the memories of his most divine love. In this relationship the burden is on her, the blame on him. Should she choose to get involved in his game of emotional Monopoly, then he should at least be fair and make sure that she's the banker.

Pisces man with Virgo woman

She is quiet, shy and very sensible. He is chaos personified, dreamy-eyed and lost in fantasy. He has a mind that seems to be travelling in too many different directions. On the other hand, she thinks straight ahead and doesn't get distracted by emotional considerations.

She may find his daydreams fascinating. However, she'll probably choke and splutter over the constant confusion he lives in. She loves to have her time organized, while he can't commit himself 10 seconds into the future. She feels secure when she can create a premeditated order; he takes spontaneity to the most peculiar extremes.

After a time she will probably watch her patience dwindle as she starts to realize how easily he can turn the romance into a kind of riot. Meanwhile, his attention span has probably wandered and is wondering when he's going to meet his next heart-throb.

Pisces man with Libra woman

He is a sentimental character who will send her soaring past the limits of her logic. He'll make her feel she's the first woman he's ever wooed and the only one he ever wants to. Together they'll enter into a dreamlike life where love becomes a drug more debilitating than the fruits of the poppy. Emotionally, they both might be coming from similar places. However, how they approach life is different enough to create frictions. Miss Libra wants a man she can lean on. He also wants someone to lean on, so if she leans on him, they could well topple over. However, if she's willing to bypass emotional support for simple companionship and doesn't mind enduring the regular assortment of murky moods, it may be worth a try. She may end up with a bad back, however, because he can be a heavy load, but whatever makes her happy is worth a little physical sacrifice.

Pisces man with Scorpio woman

He'll treat her like a drug, but she's a woman and wants to be treated like one. That is the beginning of their problems but not the end.

Sexually, he is the passive sort and in love a sea of

emotion. He prefers the dream of her distant approach far more than her personal appearance. Emotionally, she is serious, while he is sentimental. She is a strong survivor. He is weak, snivelling and sometimes whiny.

He is looking for both a movie star and a mother. If she happens to fit both roles and wants to play them, she's got you – as long as she doesn't mind sharing him with a few others. She will know about the others because when he's being unfaithful he's careless enough to make her trip over the evidence. No matter how devious he may think he is, she can see straight through him, and when she does she won't hang around long, unless she is completely smitten.

Pisces man with Sagittarius woman

He is sentimental and totally divorced from reality. She is impulsive, chaotic and conscious that there must be something that she is missing. Well, she should take a longer look, because it's not him. She is so flighty that she needs a strong hand to grab her by the neck and ground her. His is limp, probably clammy and so flexible that it feels like it's made of foam. Together, they can take many sensational side trips into the world of the paranormal. However, in the daylight, under the bustling burdens of day-to-day responsibilities, such as paying the rent, he is of little or no help. She might consider being friends with him, but shouldn't consider marriage unless she wants to play mama.

Pisces man with Capricorn woman

At first, he will seem romantic and sentimental, but on closer inspection he appears weak and wishy-washy. He has a hard time dealing with the day-to-day world, while she thrives in a competitive environment. His mind is floating somewhere above the clouds, but hers is rooted firmly on the earth. She finds his ultimate objectives vague, his emotions inconstant and his approach to life definitely escapist. Miss Capricorn is a no-nonsense person who doesn't have time for adolescent instabilities in an adult whose hair is turning grey. Her attitude is either shape up or ship out. His is take me or leave me, but don't irritate me. Any way you look at it his way is not her way, unless she likes giving generously and getting precious little in return.

Pisces man with Aquarius woman

She lives in the future; he often gets stuck in the past. She is friendly, yet detached, whereas he is more aloof and sentimental. She scatters her feelings among dozens of people, while he nurtures his in private places. They are both so different that they seem to be travelling in opposite directions. She needs change and activity, while he is content with the status quo. She gets inflamed by social injustice, while he prefers to pass the time dreaming about Utopia. She demands honesty for any committed relationship, but he believes that honesty is not always the best policy. Also, she is about as romantic as a dentist extracting a tooth, while he is intensely sentimental and sometimes a little wishy-washy. She has no patience for his armchair observations, and he has no tolerance for her perpetual curiosity. Any relationship more serious than a partnership at backgammon is sure to create mutual irritations that are more than a little electric.

Monthly and Daily Guides

JANUARY

The Sun will be digging its way through the earthy sign of Capricorn up until the 21st. This is the area of your chart devoted to team effort as well as acquaintances and friends, therefore it looks as if it's going to be an extremely sociable month and one when people you know well might be making promising introductions to the opposite sex.

From the 21st onwards the Sun will be moving into Aquarius and that is the secretive area of your chart. For reasons best known to yourself, you may be 'hiding away' or simply just beavering away in the background and possibly making plans for the future. Your instincts are at their best so for heaven's sake don't ignore them Pisces, because you do this frequently and end up chastising yourself.

For the majority of the month Mercury will be in earthy Capricorn, so increasing your chances of meeting new people. You may be attracted to those who come from very different backgrounds from yourself, or perhaps people who are a good deal younger. Well, it all helps to make life interesting, doesn't it?

Venus will be in Aquarius between 5th and 29th and because of this you need to watch out. You always do, of course, possess a secretive side to your character and this is enhanced particularly where your love affairs are concerned. Maybe you are involved with someone who already has a mate which could involve a degree of 'keeping your head down', but because you are such a highly strung person you must ask yourself whether you really need such aggravation. If you can answer that question honestly, then you may be prevented from doing something that you will certainly regret.

Mars remains in Libra until the 26th, therefore it won't pay you to be too aggressive with officials or bureaucrats. Naturally, we all feel like giving them a piece of our minds from time to time, but right now you really can't afford to antagonize them, believe you me. Mars in this placing also suggests that you may be a little too aggressive with people you are financially dependent upon, and it certainly won't pay you to tell your boss exactly how he should be doing his job.

There's really not a great deal wrong with this month that cannot be cured by caution and so it's up to you to sidestep the pitfalls that have been mentioned. Now look at the *Daily Guides* for further information.

FRIDAY 1st   Mercury is in a difficult aspect with Jupiter, and because of this there is no point in you relying on advice from other people because they will not be seeing the picture as clearly as your good self. Where romance is concerned, there seems to be almost too much fun, maybe you have a number of admirers. Well, this is one day when you could be found out.

SATURDAY 2nd   Today is the day of the Full Moon and it occurs in the watery sign of Cancer. Oh dear! This suggests either a problem in a newly made relationship or perhaps a social occasion which has been cancelled. Whichever applies you could be feeling sorry for yourself, but come on Pisces, life is full of ups and downs and this is only for 24 hours.

SUNDAY 3rd   You may be in an overly cautious mood and therefore won't like taking a strong stance until you've weighed up every point of view. Despite this, however, other planetary activity suggests that you can rely on your own instincts to cope with whatever life throws at you, so think positively and push ahead.

MONDAY 4th   This is certainly not a day to assume that other people understand what you have in mind, no matter how clear things may be to you. Today's stars suggest you should be vigilant in even the most straightforward of exchanges and conversations, otherwise you run the risk of misunderstandings which could ruin your day, which would be a pity.

TUESDAY 5th   Venus is in a beautiful aspect with your ruling planet, Neptune, and because of this you are at your most attractive, both physically and mentally, and can literally charm the birds from the trees. If you want a time for doing anything important, whether it be professional or personal, then this is the day to do it, so make the most of it, or you could regret it later on.

WEDNESDAY 6th   Don't let your sweetly sentimental

nature get the better of the more down-to-earth side of your personality. Being practical may mean you must let go of illusions about certain people, but you could find that you like them even more when you see them in the uncompromising light of reality.

THURSDAY 7th If you're honest with yourself, then you will admit that there are times when you can be a little bit naive, this is because you sometimes like to think people are being honest when they're really not. Usually, this wouldn't create too many problems, but on this day it is vital that you take what other people say with a liberal pinch of salt or face putting yourself in some kind of jeopardy.

FRIDAY 8th Whatever you do, don't let your own doubts or the uncooperative attitude of certain people stop you from tackling those issues that you want to get off your chest. First, organize your thoughts, then remind yourself that it is only their support you seek and not necessarily their agreement to every detail of what you are doing.

SATURDAY 9th You may have right on your side, but that doesn't mean you should avoid organizing your thoughts or getting your evidence together before confronting people who are opposed to you. When all is said and done, however, getting the result you want may turn out to be more a matter of luck than logic.

SUNDAY 10th Someone close to you seems not only to be unwilling to take responsibility for their actions, but they become expert at passing the buck as well. You can grumble about this all you like, but you can achieve far more if you address your objections to offenders directly, outlining exactly what you want.

MONDAY 11th Don't let the fact that other people seem uninterested, or determined to create obstacles, stop you from pursuing interests that are dear to your heart. Not only are your efforts likely to be rewarded, but this day's aspects suggest that you could yet sway others to your way of thinking.

TUESDAY 12th Even the most easy-going of Pisces has an overprotective streak when it comes to loved ones, so much so that any hint that they are unhappy can get you worked up. Before you go into overdrive, however, make sure that their problems haven't been caused by a simple misunderstanding.

WEDNESDAY 13th Venus is in a beautiful aspect with Uranus, and so during this particular day you will be prone to many sudden inspirations which are very ingenious indeed, so push ahead. You must have the confidence to let other people in on what you are thinking, otherwise somebody else may thunder past you and steal the glory that is rightfully yours. It's nice to be a modest person, Pisces, but you can overdo it.

THURSDAY 14th The Sun is in a beautiful aspect with Jupiter, so certainly where professional matters are concerned you have a great deal of confidence and a certain amount of good luck too. Clearly then, this a time for putting some of those plans you have been mulling over for quite some time into action, and as soon as possible.

FRIDAY 15th The Sun clashes with Mars, therefore when it comes to your hard-earned cash you could be unbelievably extravagant. But despite the fact you are spending a great deal this doesn't necessarily mean that you'll be getting good value for your money. A time for a certain amount of self-control, or you could rue this 24 hours.

SATURDAY 16th Sometimes what's really important about situations can come to light in the most peculiar way. The developments indicated by today's stars may be unsettling, but they will shake up those who have been behaving irrationally.

SUNDAY 17th Today is the day of the New Moon and it falls in the earthy sign of Capricorn. There's likely to be some news in connection with your friends and acquaintances, perhaps new friends in your social circle, so get out this evening and keep a high profile, you'll certainly be glad that you did as this will encourage romance.

MONDAY 18th There is one thing to be said for the emotional upheaval that has erupted around you recently which is at least you now know what others are really feeling. The air has been cleared around a certain sensitive matter and there's no need to be so coy about it any more.

TUESDAY 19th Mars is in a difficult aspect with Saturn, therefore there may be some kind of disappointment where cash matters are concerned. Perhaps a cheque fails to arrive on time, or if it does, then possibly it is less than you were anticipating. Don't feel sorry for yourself and be as philosophical as you can, after all, we can't always have what we want – unfortunately.

WEDNESDAY 20th For some time you have avoided raising sensitive issues, fearing that doing so would not only achieve nothing but might irritate those whose goodwill you rely on. Now though, you must speak out. Although they may react only a little, it will not necessarily mean that you have been ignored.

THURSDAY 21st No one respects the freedom of others more than you do, but it would be unwise to take chances on friends, family or colleagues placing their own interpretation on what you've said. Questioning them now may seem excessive, but what's revealed when you do will make you glad you did.

FRIDAY 22nd The Sun is in a beautiful aspect with your ruling planet, Neptune. This means that you have all the confidence in the world, therefore push ahead in whichever direction you feel could do with some of your attention. Certainly, if you are fancy-free, keep in the thick of all the action this evening because others will be drawn to you like moths around a flame.

SATURDAY 23rd You sometimes feel you are struggling on to no avail, but be assured that if you can just keep putting one foot in front of the other, then you will earn the respect of those whose judgement you trust. Loyalty is more important than surrounding yourself with people who only tell you the good news. Also, don't blunder about, but move steadily and you will avoid minor accidents.

SUNDAY 24th Sorting out your cash is requiring just a touch more push than you had expected, but this may be the last hurdle for a while, so just knuckle down to what is required. Watch that you are not pushing past the limits of your energy, because you need to be fit as well as secure. Luckily, you seem to be talking to good effect to close companions.

MONDAY 25th The stars fill you with get up and go and you are ready for action, and quite likely to get heated with anyone who obstructs your path. However, you have to control your irritability and channel it into something more specific, maybe a job you've overlooked. Forget frivolities and indulgences for a day and try to be self-disciplined.

TUESDAY 26th Mercury will be moving into the air sign of Aquarius, which is the rather private part of your chart and so you will be spending a good deal of time with your own personal thoughts over the next few weeks. Maybe you have propositions to consider, or perhaps a decision in your love life, whichever applies you'll do the right thing as long as you take sufficient time.

WEDNESDAY 27th There's a strong likelihood that

you are cross and crotchety because of one situation which makes you feel you are trying to sail ahead with the anchor down. But sometimes being held back allows you to reserve energy for future situations. You can also use this quiet time to throw yourself into reorganizing at home. It may not be a great laugh, but you will feel virtuous in the end.

THURSDAY 28th   Trying to get close companions to understand exactly what is on your mind is no easy matter. You feel you are continually having to go over and over the same ground with little progress. However, practise makes perfect, they always say, so don't get discouraged. You have wonderfully dynamic friends and allies around as well.

FRIDAY 29th   The day ahead is likely to be one of solid hard work. You will not be suffering fools gladly, and the loyal support of one close partner will certainly be helping you. Talking about money will increase the chances of fattening your wallet, so make sure you have all of the facts at your disposal.

SATURDAY 30th   Venus will be moving into your own sign, which is good news because for the next couple of weeks you'll be physically looking your best and will be attracting other people to you. It could be an important time for your emotional life, too, and if you are single, you should keep your eyes peeled for some interesting prospects. Those already in a relationship may be thinking about making that all important commitment.

SUNDAY 31st   Today is the day of the Full Moon and it occurs in the fiery sign of Leo. This is the area of your chart devoted to routine work which, while not exactly congenial, will be taking you towards your ultimate goal, therefore don't find excuses to procrastinate because you will be delaying the arrival of rewards in the future.

FEBRUARY

The Sun will be coasting along in Aquarius up until the 18th, and so up to this date you'll be quite happy to keep yourself to yourself, make plans for the future and exercise your intuitions on new people you meet. Fortunately, once the 18th has passed the Sun moves into your sign and then it is up to you to step into the limelight and gather the rewards that are due to you, as well as keeping a high profile and pushing ahead with whatever is important to you.

Mercury, too, will be entering your sign on the 13th, enlivening that grey matter of yours so that you'll have many wondrous inspirations which will impress everybody around, just as long as you let them know what you are thinking. This is not a time for being too secretive.

Venus remains in your sign until the 21st, so you are still looking good, feeling good and drawing an admiring crowd. If you're thinking of making important emotional decisions, you couldn't have a better time for doing just that. From the 22nd onwards Venus will be moving into the cash area of your life, which really cannot be too bad, because this brings gains through cooperation with other people as well as through arts, partnerships and goodwill.

Mind you, it is also possible that you may be inclined to spoil yourself and other people from time to time, but as long as you keep this within the bounds of reason then there isn't any reason why you shouldn't.

Mars continues to coast along in Scorpio for the entire month, so don't be too quarrelsome or disagreeable when you are introduced to new people, particularly if they come from foreign lands. For some, there may be a sexual fling which you may believe is going to be the love of your life, but I'm afraid you'll be disappointed. Still, there's no reason why you shouldn't exercise your sexuality from time to time and the worst thing you can do is feel guilty about it.

Now look at the *Daily Guides* for further information.

MONDAY 1st The Sun and Uranus are in a beautiful aspect, which suggests that you will be filled with inspiration and brilliant ideas, but don't keep them to yourself Pisces, otherwise you'll be playing your own worst enemy, which you do from time to time. Anything that happens to complete the unexpected should be investigated before rejected and that includes people as well as opportunities.

TUESDAY 2nd You know you want to take decisions into your own hands, but not everyone appears to be willing to dance to your tune, so you may just have to be self-sufficient. Go your own way and do not be distracted by anyone else's whims. Your security is of paramount importance. Where there is a will there is a way, and you can push through problems without any difficulty if you have a mind to.

WEDNESDAY 3rd You are trying to aim in too many directions at once, so you need to damp down your energy to focus on what is really in your own best interest. You seem to be determinedly pruning out anything in your life that will not be useful in the future. Don't expect instant results, but you are heading in the right direction which is comforting.

THURSDAY 4th The Sun today is in a beautiful aspect with Mercury, therefore everybody around you, both at work and at home, will be in high spirits and so if you want a time for sorting out past differences or asking for one or two little favours, then that day has arrived.

FRIDAY 5th Venus is in a difficult aspect with Pluto, therefore you need to take care of how you approach other people because by making too many demands you could irritate them and cause hostilities. If you have anything important planned for this evening, it might be a good idea to do some double-checking, but nothing is likely to be straightforward in this area of life just now.

SATURDAY 6th The day ahead will be a hard-working one. You will not be suffering fools gladly for a change, and the loyal support of one close friend or partner will help. Talking about money will increase income, so make sure you have all the facts at your disposal when you do.

SUNDAY 7th You are more attuned than most to accepting life the way it is. So hang on in there through the patches when no one seems inclined to indulge your wishes or hopes. In the end, you will emerge stronger, wiser and better informed. You know that joint finances and, indeed, all cooperative ventures in your life will take time to settle, so be patient.

MONDAY 8th Older friends or team-mates may be rather cool or objective, but they are pointing you in sensible directions. You need to be more aware of what is going on with one close partner because everyone needs to pull together at the moment. Placating their disagreements may be the first move before you can push any further ahead.

TUESDAY 9th Slogging up hill murmuring unkind words about lack of cooperation all round may be your instinctive response to what life is offering you right now. But really, if you have any sense, you would see that this is the perfect opportunity to prove your independence. Put your back into your schemes and do it your way.

WEDNESDAY 10th No one doubts that your enthusiasm and physical energy are high, but you know you cannot just be flamboyant or theatrical. You also have to show a sensible resolve to older companions or those whose judgement you can trust. It is clearly the time to push yourself into making practical decisions. Do a little well, rather than too much badly.

THURSDAY 11th Sorting out joint finances has been a bugbear over the past few years, but you are making steady progress. You need to keep persuading yourself of this if you feel there is an imminent setback. Over the long haul, you are laying very solid foundations domestically and financially, so keep doing what you do best – sorting out the details.

FRIDAY 12th   If you feel you are not standing on very solid ground, then you need to just float along until you are clearer about what you want at home. There are deceptive influences around which suggests your judgement is not good and that you may be worrying about something that will never happen. Be kind and sensitive to yourself as well as gentle with loved ones.

SATURDAY 13th   Get some peace and quiet when you can, then you will suddenly discover that you have your audience back. For a few days you have felt as if no one was really hearing you, which was unsettling. You fully intend to make up for lost time, which may confuse close companions as you rattle away at high speed. Spending money on luxuries does you good.

SUNDAY 14th   Close partners should be ready to give you support, which will improve your spirits, though you may have to shift ground to keep them happy. Make sure you are doing everything possible to pamper yourself as well. You're looking good and feeling chirpy, so you should be able to attract a few compliments. Make no cash decisions just for the moment.

MONDAY 15th   Whatever the muddles and question marks you know that you want to start discussing long-term plans. Younger friends in particular will be nudging you out of a rut and telling you to look ahead, not backwards. Although your love life leaves a little to be desired you can still enjoy the private moments.

TUESDAY 16th   Today is the day of the New Moon and it occurs in the airy sign of Aquarius. Although you may be feeling more optimistic and even excited, you may not have any clear idea as to exactly why. It seems that you are picking up vibrations of the good times that lie ahead and you should hug these to yourself in order to keep you in a positive frame of mind. As always with New Moons, you can begin something new.

WEDNESDAY 17th   Today the Sun will be lining up with Saturn and so, although there may be a delay where a romantic or social occasion is concerned and providing you can contain your impatience and excitability, then everything will go according to plan in the fullness of time. In the meantime it will pay to keep yourself as busy as possible.

THURSDAY 18th   Mercury is in a difficult aspect with Pluto, so the stars are suggesting that other people may want to make some dramatic changes. This may be to their appearance, the way they are leading their life or their future plans, and if you stand in their way, then don't be surprised if you are swept to one side. It might be a good idea to cooperate.

FRIDAY 19th   Now is the time to show your wit, wisdom and brilliant ways with words. There's no doubt that you have a good many facts and figures at your fingertips

and you intend to spray them in all directions. Your
friends also want your light-hearted sense of humour,
so be sociable, frivolous and flirtatious when you can
find the right company.

SATURDAY 20th   You are looking good and feeling
very bouncy and optimistic and determinedly wearing
your best smile, so consequently you are definitely top of
quite a few popularity polls. You have been hiding away
recently, sorting out some confidential matters, but now
you can spread your wings a little and fly higher. Talk
to friends who are living some distance away.

SUNDAY 21st   Friends are enormously supportive and
optimistic, so lap up the attention and enjoy their compliments. You know you need to sort out joint finances and
to talk to loved ones about more confidential matters in
the next few days, but you need to find the right balance
because you dislike being tied down too much.

MONDAY 22nd   A word of praise makes you blush
with delight and there could even be a small present coming your way, so prepare to look appreciative.
Passions are running deep but that does not mean you
cannot kick your heels up once in a while. Make sure
you are being open with close partners. They need to
know what is on your mind, which is usually a mystery
to them.

TUESDAY 23rd   You are packing in every last moment
of enjoyment, where possible, because you have a sinking

feeling that you will have to concentrate more on work during the coming days. There will be practical details to attend to and becoming a good deal more efficient is vital. Any health queries can be happily answered if you just ask the right advisor.

WEDNESDAY 24th Eating well and generally indulging yourself has made the past few days rather easier to cope with. You are especially pleased to be on the receiving end of a wonderful present from someone close. All of a sudden your sense of humour surfaces so that loved ones will be kept well entertained. Make sure you are able to avoid any tedious chores.

THURSDAY 25th Sparkling in the spotlight, you are clearly having a great deal of fun and entertainment. No one parties quite like you, but you also find time to talk to loved ones. You need to step back a little over the next few days to ponder on what comes next. The more you voice your feelings to the family the easier you will find it to understand yourself.

FRIDAY 26th Home life is sweet and your appetite is doing very well, so there may be a minor expansion going on. The planetary setup today will speed up life considerably. Enjoy yourself when you can because the next few weeks will be varied and you will find it difficult to find time even to pause for breath.

SATURDAY 27th The day ahead will be slightly vague at home, but happy and successful at work, and healthy too. Be sensible about cash matters, because heavier responsibilities look likely to arrive some time next month.

SUNDAY 28th The Moon's position in Leo may prove to be something of a drain on your energies as well as your enthusiasm. Just for one day pull in the reins and do a little bit of contemplating or planning for the future. If you act right now, you may not be doing yourself justice, so it would be a good idea to hole up and even be a little lazy.

MARCH

This month, of course, the Sun will be coasting along in your sign up until the 20th, and because of this you have more faith in yourself and your appearance, and a happy smile will be drawing other people to you. Anything which is connected with your own wellbeing or ambitions should be pushed during this time, otherwise you'll regret it for quite some time to come.

From the 20th onwards the Sun will be moving into the cash area of your chart, which is no bad thing, because this will encourage you to save and conserve rather than spend as if there were no tomorrow. You may also be sorting out complicated financial problems at the speed of light.

Mercury is in a changeable mood this month and has a tendency to keep popping in and out of your sign. This is likely to make you restless and so any opportunities to meet new faces or go to new places should be snapped up as soon as possible. Some of you may be signing important documents or going on interviews and either or both will be successful. Keep a notepad and pen handy because ideas need jotting down before they disappear into the mists of time.

Venus continues to coast along in the financial area of life up until the 17th, and because of this you will still be drawn to spending on luxuries and on pleasing other people too. Luckily, after this date, Venus will be moving on into Taurus, throwing a happy glow over any casual relationships that are made at this time.

Mars continues its retrograde movement through the water sign of Scorpio, therefore, late month in particular, you must be especially careful when in the company of people who come from vastly different backgrounds or countries from yourself. It won't take very much to upset them, so get out that Pisces charm, which I know you have, and use it to good effect.

Now look at the *Daily Guides* for further information.

MONDAY 1st The Sun is in a beautiful aspect with Mars, which won't do your financial situation any harm whatsoever. There may be some opportunities for you to fatten your bank account, or perhaps money that is owed finally rolls in, whichever applies it is likely to bring a smile to your face.

TUESDAY 2nd Today is the day of the Full Moon and it occurs in the earthy sign of Virgo. This is your opposite sign in the zodiac and it is a placing which is likely to make people who are closest to you rather forgetful, bad-tempered or uncooperative, or maybe even all three. If a relationship of yours is in trouble, this is the one moment in the month when someone may decide to call it to a halt and it might just as well be you.

WEDNESDAY 3rd The less you have to do, the easier your day. Avoid careless purchases otherwise you may have to return them later. As communication and travel don't seem to be as simple as they should be tonight, steer clear of trouble spots and touchy topics and in this way you'll be saving yourself a good deal of aggravation.

THURSDAY 4th Go with the flow and don't pin yourself to a plan that's too rigid. The more you try to get things organized and settled, or to set ideas in stone, the more opposition you will encounter. This evening you can certainly look forward to a time that has a lot of sparkle. You and a partner may suddenly start talking about something that's been 'off limits' lately.

FRIDAY 5th You may start your day feeling dreamy and lazy because the stars are doing their utmost to suppress your physical energy. Try not to read too much into a partner's mood, you could be misinterpreting them. This evening could be a special time for lovers, but be careful not to shut out other people when they're expecting to be included or kept up to date with your plans.

SATURDAY 6th This is a good day for playing a spectator rather than being a participator. There seems to be a laid-back atmosphere which is better suited to being a touch lazy and not getting into anything too serious. Keep everything light and easy. Remember, too, that kind, unselfish thoughts and deeds mean a great deal.

You seem to be thinking of anyone but yourself, although you could be tempted to splash out on an unplanned purchase. Try to keep to your budget – you know it makes sense.

SUNDAY 7th If your job requires imagination, then today is fine, but if you need bundles of vitality, it could be harder going. Make sure you get some rest throughout this period. This evening your social life kicks into gear and you'll be spoiled for choice over events. You could have cause for a celebration in connection with a special person.

MONDAY 8th The Moon is stirring up the travel area of your chart and you'll want to get away from your usual haunts. You could be torn between two choices this evening, though, so go with the lighter, easier one and avoid people who tug at those guilt strings of yours. You can be easy to manipulate but make sure this isn't the case today.

TUESDAY 9th The opening of a new door at work, or within the family, seems to warm things up and spread a great air of optimism around you. You could be feeling pleased with something that's very much 'your idea', and if you want to keep it that way, it might be a good idea not to be quite so confiding with other people.

WEDNESDAY 10th It's possible that the stars may be sapping your energy and perhaps slowing down your thoughts which keep drifting back to the past. You should avoid too heavy a schedule at this time, because it simply won't sit comfortably on your shoulders. Slowly does it seems to be the motto right now.

THURSDAY 11th The stars seem to cheer you up in a very satisfactory way and you could hear hoped-for words from a loved one. There may be an awkwardness with travel and long-distance conversations, but take heart, things are likely to be more settled than they appear to be on the surface.

FRIDAY 12th This evening seems to be routine with nothing fantastic or awesomely difficult occurring. It also looks promising for letting other people entertain you and for enjoying a spot of relaxation, although complex aspects cause strange atmospheres around your relationships. What you must do is to aim to keep things simple, and if you play your astrological cards in the right order, you will find that you will be propelled into the arms of somebody you care a great deal for.

SATURDAY 13th You could benefit either financially or emotionally through somebody else. There will be some pressure on you to do more than you really want to – don't. Try to organize your day to suit your own needs and then it will be a satisfactory one.

SUNDAY 14th You are likely to be thinking many dreamy thoughts, caught up in memories and conjuring up visions of the future as the stars weave a spell around you. Family arrangements are likely to go better tomorrow rather than today, so try to plan accordingly if you possibly can.

MONDAY 15th Only those closest to you know how one word spoken at a vulnerable moment can trigger unsettling doubts. While reviewing situations may be a wise move, the stars do suggest there's a certain amount of illusion around. Because of this, it's likely that matters will not be as grim as they may seem on the surface.

TUESDAY 16th Other people seem eager to get plans made and the future arranged, but in such affairs haste can be as unwise as doing nothing. Never was this truer than right now because no one, let alone you, can be sure of the direction in which you will want to go on this particular day.

WEDNESDAY 17th Today is the day of the New Moon and luckily it falls in your sign, therefore you will look good, feel great and be ready to turn the world around on its axis. People may wonder what has come over such a timid sensitive person as your good self, so they may very well be going back to the drawing board and trying to work you out all over again. As always with New Moons, it's a great time for starting anything new.

THURSDAY 18th You may in theory be aware of the limits of your responsibility, but your feelings are considerably less cut and dried. Consequently, unless you are careful, you could be taken advantage of by those who are trying to deflect the blame from themselves and laying it at your doorstep.

FRIDAY 19th Venus is in a beautiful aspect with Saturn, and so there's a happy and harmonious glow over your friendship circle. If you need any advice or assistance, this is the ideal day for asking for it because nobody can deny you.

SATURDAY 20th While you're not exactly shy, there are things that, for various reasons, you haven't felt able to say. Now you wish you had, but fortunately the stars right now indicate this is an ideal moment to express those ideas, and doing so could bring unexpected rewarding exchanges.

SUNDAY 21st Venus is in a difficult aspect with Neptune. It's likely therefore that your judgement is completely off and your imagination may run away with you and you will exaggerate the importance of minor setbacks. The best thing you can do is not take yourself too seriously until this day has passed and try to avoid overindulgence this evening.

MONDAY 22nd You may begin this day feeling miserable and convinced that there's no way out of the problems you face, but don't despair. Unexpected developments either improve your position or introduce opportunities that will enable you to dispense with issues once and for all.

TUESDAY 23rd You may assume that partners or colleagues are keeping track of details or watching the financial side of developments, but don't bet on it. Their approach to such matters is likely to be lackadaisical and unless you keep track of developments their inattentiveness could land you in difficulties.

WEDNESDAY 24th Don't let your need to ensure the happiness of friends, loved ones and, most of all, partners, mean that certain issues are ignored. If you have already raised them and have received no response, then you could easily misinterpret that silence as a lack of interest. It is far more likely that other people simply don't understand what you are hoping for, or were expecting from them.

THURSDAY 25th Now that the stars which brought to a head issues involving domestic matters or your working life have moved on you can consider your options. Don't take too long to decide, however, because others may misinterpret this as meaning that you're happy with things as they are.

FRIDAY 26th There are times when no matter how clear you are in conversation with those you live or work with, they seem almost determined to misunderstand you. You can do little about their attitude but by refusing to allow them to aggravate you ensures you retain the upper hand.

SATURDAY 27th It may appear that you have all the time in the world to settle matters that involve a combination of finances and loved ones. But things are moving quickly, so much so that unless you lay groundwork for remedies over the next few days, developments could sweep opportunities away.

SUNDAY 28th You can't completely ignore the setbacks of the past few days, but you don't need to take them too seriously. In fact, patience brings its own rewards today, as developments that accompany the aspects turn the tide in your favour.

MONDAY 29th For reasons of a strategic nature, you seem to have been unable to speak out as you would like to about certain matters. Not only does being more forthright become possible soon, it is actually essential that you make your views known.

TUESDAY 30th The Sun is in a beautiful aspect with Jupiter, and because of this there is certainly a rosy glow over your professional hopes and plans. You must persuade yourself to push ahead with everything that is important to you, because to miss out now will be regretted at a later date.

WEDNESDAY 31st Today is the day of the Full Moon and it occurs in the airy sign of Libra. It's possible then that somebody you are financially dependent upon may be going through a rather rough patch, but if you can offer or help with encouragement and perhaps your love too, then they will be replenished, revitalized and ready to get back into the world and resume the fight.

APRIL

The Sun will be coasting along in the cash area of your life up until the 20th, which is most certainly what you need right now. You are provided with approximately three weeks for saving instead of spending as you generally prefer to do. From the 21st onwards this centre of our universe will be moving into the earth sign of Taurus, placing the emphasis on intellectual affairs as well as short journeys which will become more frequent.

Mercury will also be moving into the cash area of your chart on the 18th, so you can certainly gain from interviews, negotiations, new ideas and perhaps from new people.

Venus moves into Gemini on the 13th, throwing a happy congenial glow over property and family affairs. It's likely that after this date you will be entertaining at home far more than is usually the case and doing so with a certain amount of panache and style, which will cause admiration and praise.

Mars continues its retrograde movement through Scorpio, therefore you must remain cordial and welcoming to strangers who enter your social circle and perhaps your home. You may not agree with everything they say but there is a right and wrong way of telling them so, which I'm sure you are capable of recognizing.

Now look at the *Daily Guides* for further information.

THURSDAY 1st The Sun is in a beautiful aspect with Jupiter, giving you far more confidence and 'get up and go' where work matters are concerned. Just for once you're not content to sit in the wings and allow everybody else to gallop off with the glory, especially as you know that you have been the instigator of their every move. Time to draw attention to yourself then, rather than remaining in the wings.

FRIDAY 2nd The reasons behind other people's decisions

are unlikely to have much to do with reality. That being the case, you can either debate issues, while knowing how futile this is, or save your fire for a time when your arguments are going to receive a better hearing. The choice is, of course, entirely up to you.

SATURDAY 3rd One moment you are caring and sympathetic, the next you are as tough as old boots. The stars hint that misunderstandings at home will require subtle, sensitive handling. No wonder you are feeling puzzled about which approach to use. Luckily, you have initiative and energy, so use them wisely. Be flexible.

SUNDAY 4th Hard work and ambition can make you feel isolated, and you suddenly begin to crave the company of friends. If you are having a minor identity crisis, just sit quietly until the moment passes. Sorting out tensions at home will demand all of your concentration for a day or so, then, surrounded by supportive faces, you can start planning for the long term.

MONDAY 5th You may appear to be flexible on the surface, but you're never really happy to let other people make your decisions for you. You feel perplexed by many questions. Hold your fire until inspiration strikes. In the meantime, you have confidential negotiations on the go with professional or emotional partners. Keep at it until you find long-term solutions that seem fair to everyone.

TUESDAY 6th Home and family have been of great support recently, but a close friend is being evasive. You aren't clear what sort of commitment they want either.

Grit your teeth and force yourself to work independently. The reward for hard work is usually more of the same, but it's doing you good. There will be party invitations, jokes and even flirtations in the future.

WEDNESDAY 7th   You may be feeling woolly headed and incapable of stringing your words together, but don't worry. Just muddle along and avoid making too many decisions, because you may take a wrong turn. Save your energy as a money matter may crop up in the not too distant future. The stars are beginning to push you to a new phase when things will begin to look up again.

THURSDAY 8th   The planetary setup today will give you a flow of wit, wisdom and ideas about work that will win the respect of other people. If only they knew how much uncertainty you were hiding inside. Find time to be alone and reflect. no one doubts your commitment but you have to find a balance that allows time for selfish concerns.

FRIDAY 9th   Too much work and too little appreciation are rather wearing on the body and spirit, but don't be despondent. You have accomplished a good deal recently and just a few finishing touches are needed before you enjoy more support and cooperation.

SATURDAY 10th   For the moment, stamina and patience will see you through whatever life throws at you, and soon the stars will lift your spirits and you will feel wanted again. It might be a good idea to cut loose from uncooperative workmates, but do it graciously.

SUNDAY 11th   A time of variety, challenge and intriguing encounters has been entertaining, but you are starting to feel like slowing down. Talk to loved ones or family to clear your mind. If necessary, step back to give yourself some thinking time. You will have duties to perform in the days ahead and a serious approach will earn respect. On the whole, though, you want to stand clear of the fray.

MONDAY 12th   Get to grips on cash matters and avoid sentimental decisions. Being a water sign you find practical details a bore, but now is the time to anchor yourself firmly to reality. If you don't do so now, a situation will force you to do so in the not too distant future.

TUESDAY 13th   Friends may not be the best advisors at the moment, so what you need to do is find hard-headed experts to guide you along your way. Tie up loose ends at work because you are moving into a slower patch when achievements may not happen as quickly as you'd like.

WEDNESDAY 14th   You may not be sure where you're going, but you definitely know what you're leaving behind. It's likely that the past few days may have been something of a struggle, rather like wading through treacle. Friends may not seem entirely solid in their support but they will be 'there' when you need them the most.

THURSDAY 15th   All the fun, games and flirtations of the past few weeks have left you wanting more, but everything has its price and now you're facing a patch of hard work, fidgeting around with details and being efficient.

FRIDAY 16th There is a beautiful New Moon in the fiery sign of Aries and this, of course, is the cash area of your chart which must be good news. Either you are receiving a belated present or perhaps a fresh source of income is beckoning and if so, don't question it too much. You can always do that at a later date when you're fully aware of the situations and people involved.

SATURDAY 17th Make sure that your health is on top form since you need the stamina to keep up with the chores which require your attention. Close mates may be rather grumpy and try to push you into being more realistic, while this scheme may sound exciting try to wind down just a little.

SUNDAY 18th Are you absolutely happy about your financial position? What bothers you is more of an emotional disappointment than a practical anxiety. Luckily, the speed of life will whizz you away from any worries, but don't make decisions or commitments when your head is in the clouds.

MONDAY 19th Don't let your need to ensure the happiness of friends, loved ones and, most of all, partners mean that certain issues are ignored. If you have already raised these and received no response, you could easily misinterpret that silence as a lack of interest. It's far more likely that others simply don't understand what you were hoping for or were expecting from them.

TUESDAY 20th Only those closest to you know how one word spoken at a vulnerable moment can trigger unsettling doubts. While revealing situations may be wise, the planetary setup today indicates that issues are unlikely to be as grim as they seem.

WEDNESDAY 21st Venus is in a war with Pluto, and because of this you must make sure that if you should run across new faces, either at work or at home, you remain affable and accommodating. Right now you could give an unfortunate impression of either remoteness or arrogance.

THURSDAY 22nd Other people seem eager to get plans made and the future arranged, but in such matters haste can be as unwise as inaction. Never was this truer than right now because it will only be after the Full Moon on the 30th that anyone, let alone you, can be sure of the direction in which you will want to go.

FRIDAY 23rd You may in theory be aware of the limits of your responsibility, but your feelings are considerably less cut and tried. Consequently, unless you are careful, you could be taken advantage of by those who are trying to deflect the blame away from themselves and lay it at your doorstep.

SATURDAY 24th The Sun is in a difficult aspect with Neptune, and because of this you may be overconfident and verging on arrogance, which is totally unlike your usual self. Best to allow other people to step into the limelight, whilst you back them in any way that you think practical and reasonable.

SUNDAY 25th Mercury is in a beautiful aspect with Pluto, which suggests that those who are closest to you will want to make some changes. At least give them a listen before you overrule them, otherwise you will be stirring up resentment and storing up trouble for the future.

MONDAY 26th Venus is in a beautiful aspect with Uranus, so your imagination is working at full tilt and certainly where work matters are concerned you will have an original touch which will impress. Some of you, too, may be romantically involved with a colleague but make sure that ulterior motives aren't at work here.

TUESDAY 27th The Sun is in a fine aspect with Saturn, throwing a happy glow over the friendship area of your life. Because of this, if you need any help or assistance from other people, then you must gather your courage in your hands and don't be afraid to ask for it. When all's said and done, they can only say 'no', but this is most unlikely to occur.

WEDNESDAY 28th You may not be shy but there are things that, for various reasons, you haven't felt able to say but now you wish you had. However, the planetary setup today indicates that this is the ideal moment to express those ideas, and doing so could bring unexpected and rewarding exchanges.

THURSDAY 29th   You may begin today feeling miserable, convinced that there is no way out of problems you face, but don't despair. Unexpected developments either improve your position or introduce opportunities that are sufficient to enable you to deal with certain issues once and for all.

FRIDAY 30th   Today is the day of the Full Moon and it occurs in the watery sign of Scorpio. This is not the best time then for booking a holiday, or dealing with people who come from distant lands. It may also be harder for you to concentrate on intricate matters, so if it is at all possible put them to one side for the time being. You don't want to end this month on a low note.

MAY

The Sun will be coasting along in the earthy sign of Taurus up until the 20th. This is the area of your chart devoted to the mind, so concentration will be increased. It's also a possibility that you'll be taking many short trips, perhaps for little cause other than the fact that you are restless. Buying and selling can be successful, too, so don't be afraid to ask for the price that you desire.

From the 20th onwards the Sun will be moving into Gemini and that is the area of your chart devoted to property and family. These areas therefore will assume greater importance for approximately a month and, like it or not, you must attend to them.

Mercury is in a restless mood this month, but it does spend the majority of May between the 9th and 23rd in the sign of Taurus. This suggests that short trips and new beginnings may occur in connection with your financial affairs. During the last week it's likely that affairs related to brothers or sisters will be highlighted in some way.

Venus will be moving into the water sign of Cancer on the 9th. This is the area of your chart connected with children, pleasure, sports and romance. From this date onwards it certainly isn't a time to take the opposite sex too seriously. They're in a flirty mood and so are you, therefore a lot of things may be said on the spur of the moment without due thought, which may need retracting at a later date and this could be embarrassing.

Mars' retrograde movement has taken it back into the sign of Libra, which is the area of your chart that tends to represent people you are financially dependent upon and it's quite likely that they are experiencing a difficult period. They would no doubt be grateful for any support or encouragement that you can give them, so see what you can do.

Now look at the *Daily Guides* for further information.

SATURDAY 1st You may assume that partners or colleagues are keeping track of details and watching the financial side of developments, but don't bet on it. Their approach to such matters is likely to be lackadaisical and unless you keep track of developments their inattentiveness could land you in difficulties.

SUNDAY 2nd Now that the planetary setup which brought to a head issues involving domestic or work matters is over you can consider your options. Several are appealing but don't take too long to decide, because other people may misinterpret this as meaning that you're happy with things as they are, which is not true.

MONDAY 3rd There are times when no matter how clear you are in exchanges with those you live or work with they seem almost determined to misunderstand you. You can do little about their attitude, but by refusing to allow them to aggravate you ensures you retain the upper hand.

TUESDAY 4th It may appear that you have all the time in the world to settle issues that involve a combination of finances and loved ones. But things are moving quickly, so much so that unless you lay the groundwork for remedies over the next few days, developments could sweep opportunities away.

WEDNESDAY 5th You can't completely ignore the setbacks of the past few days, but you need not take them too seriously. In fact, patience brings its own rewards very soon, as developments that accompany the planetary setup turn the tide in your favour.

THURSDAY 6th Mars' retrograde movement has taken it back into the air sign of Libra, therefore it would not be a good idea to upset officials, bureaucrats and the like for a couple of weeks or so. If you do, I'm afraid you could be paying dearly for your mistake. There's a chance this evening that arguments could flare up over money, too, so plaster a sweet smile on your face and at least give other people the benefit of the doubt.

FRIDAY 7th The Sun is in a difficult aspect with Uranus, therefore those of you who are working may be prone to constant interruption and change which could lead to a degree of stress. Should you find this to be the case, then for heavens sake plan a quiet evening where you can let the troubles of the world drift away and pamper yourself just a little.

SATURDAY 8th For reasons of a strategic nature, you seem to have been unable to speak out as you would like to about certain issues. Today's planetary setup, however, not only suggests that being more forthright becomes possible, it is actually essential that you make your views known loud and clear.

SUNDAY 9th Venus will be moving into the watery sign of Cancer, and this will be providing a 'shot in the arm' to your social life as well as romance, which is likely to be flirty. You seem to be in for an enjoyable time but not one when you should take yourself or your reactions to other people too seriously.

MONDAY 10th Mercury is moving into the earthy sign of Taurus, and because of this new contacts and friends will be entering your circle over the next couple of weeks or so. Make sure you have a smile on your face and a warm welcome waiting for them because it seems that they are likely to be important to your future plans.

TUESDAY 11th During this tricky day, the reasons behind other people's decisions are unlikely to have much to do with reality. That being the case, you can either debate issues, while knowing how futile this is, or save your fire for a time when your arguments are going to receive a better hearing.

WEDNESDAY 12th Don't let a recent success stop you from making your mark in other areas, especially since you seem anxious to broaden your horizons. Today's planetary setup is enabling you to make constructive inroads into what has, until now, been just a dream. It is particularly important not to allow yourself to be discouraged by partners or those in positions of authority, because no one is a better judge of your chances of success than you.

THURSDAY 13th You seem to be in a state of limbo over a responsibility or an obligation and must now decide whether to find a way to help ease the load. Domestic and family matters will dominate your agenda and you will have no excuse for ignoring the needs of someone close. The perfect solution seldom exists, but you are advised to find a workable compromise.

FRIDAY 14th Tiny steps are not your style, giant strides suit you better, well, at this time anyway. However, care rather than haste counts on this particular day, especially when it comes to creative, family or romantic activities. The effects of a recent disappointment linger but there is nothing to be gained by bulldozing the opposition. Remember that speed only means safety when you're skating on thin ice.

SATURDAY 15th Today is the day of the New Moon

and it occurs in the earthy sign of Taurus. Because of this it will be difficult for you to sit still for very long and you'll find excuses to keep popping out. Some of you may be given the opportunity to take a short trip and you should accept as it could be lucky for you. Furthermore, this is also a good day for presenting your ideas to other people because, they'll find them quite ingenious. As always, New Moons can be used for making fresh starts.

SUNDAY 16th   The stars suggest that you are probably not feeling terribly adventurous or energetic, which is fine because you will gain more through persistence than stamina during this day. Indeed, by concentrating your efforts on business or finances you will discover that the situation is far more promising than you realized. It is up to you to prove that you are better at walking up hill than down.

MONDAY 17th   Venus is in a beautiful aspect with Saturn, and because of this you will find that friends and acquaintances are in a friendly as well as helpful frame of mind. If you need any kind of advice, then you now know where to go. Just make sure you take it on board rather than let it go in one ear and out the other.

TUESDAY 18th   Let other people waste time scoring points today – you have more important matters on your mind. You should have no shortage of ideas as how to best handle business or domestic affairs, and the stars will help you to put them to good effect. Everyone seems to think they know the answer to your problems, but the only person who really does is you.

WEDNESDAY 19th Don't allow an authority figure to undermine your faith in someone or something close to your heart. The planets today may do more to cloud than clarify, but it would be a mistake to believe that power equals wisdom. In fact, your knowledge of this person or project is greater than most, so don't be afraid to let others jockey for position while you secure your own.

THURSDAY 20th No one has the right to criticize another person's choice of friends or partners because all relationships tend to be a mystery to everyone except those concerned. Luckily, you seem to know your own mind as to the true value of a current association. However, this is not the time for inflated expectations and you would be wise to ensure that all demands are reasonable.

FRIDAY 21st The Sun will be moving into the air sign of Gemini, which is the area of your chart devoted to home, family and property. Therefore, if you need to sort out people you live with, or hunt around for your ideal home, then you're given a couple of weeks when you should be successful. Entertaining at home will be rewarding too, so don't let other people put you off from doing just that.

SATURDAY 22nd Try not to get disheartened by what you see as your ineffectuality when it comes to dealing with a family or domestic issue. Today's aspects may undermine your self-belief, but there is no disputing you are doing the best you can. Soon you'll be able to view your accomplishments from a more practical position. Count your blessings – you have plenty.

SUNDAY 23rd There's more to life than status and worldly success – as you are the first to concede. So why waste time trying to improve your image when it's the quality of your life that counts? The stars today suggest that a brilliant idea may not be all that it seems. Don't worry. Fulfilment of one kind or another looms. Just be sure that what you seek is what you want.

MONDAY 24th The longer you bury your head in the sand over a partnership, domestic or family issue, the less likely you will be to find a sensible solution. However, with today's planetary setup you must be especially careful not to overreact or read more into a situation than exists. Soon life should start becoming more relaxed and enjoyable, but you must keep a cautious eye on your health and wellbeing.

TUESDAY 25th The Sun is lining up with your ruling planet, Neptune, filling you with confidence and self-belief. This is an ideal day then for sifting through your ambitions and working out exactly what you want out of life and then to find a practical way of pushing ahead.

WEDNESDAY 26th You are in danger of losing sight of your priorities and need to recognize what really is important in your life. Today's planetary setup suggests your clarity of vision should return soon. Health, work and money problems can also be addressed, but don't expect anyone to bale you out when it's your personal input and commitment that counts. Never forget that price and value are two very different things.

THURSDAY 27th The recent upheavals at home or work have taken more out of you than you fully appreciate, but now the time has come to let bygones be bygones and to concentrate on the future. The stars today may encourage you to exaggerate the chances of a business or financial venture, but you are realistic enough to know where to draw the line. Don't be ashamed to say what you are not ashamed to think.

FRIDAY 28th It is beginning to look as if you've allowed outstanding debts to remain unpaid for far too long, so a firm reminder wouldn't go amiss. After all, you are only asking for what is due to you, so don't feel uncomfortable. Once you've satisfied your obsession for financial organization, turn your attention to your love life because it needs more attention than your bank balance.

SATURDAY 29th Those closest to you are certainly in a romantic and sentimental frame of mind, which could lead to you revisiting places that hold special memories. If you're single, you'll be drawn to those who wouldn't normally attract you, such as people who are hypersensitive and romantic, but if you insist on giving chase just make sure that you don't bruise their sensitivities, which would be all too easy for you to do.

SUNDAY 30th   Today is the day of the Full Moon and it occurs in the fiery sign of Sagittarius. This is the working area of your life where it looks as if something is coming to an end, perhaps a project or a contract. On no account should you feel insecure, although it is difficult for you not to on this day, and have faith in yourself.

MONDAY 31st   The Sun is in a difficult aspect with Pluto, therefore there may be a certain amount of upheaval or change that doesn't exactly suit you right now. Instead of panicking and becoming upset, delve a little deeper into what is going on, because when you do you may find that, after all, this has your approval.

JUNE

The Sun this month will be breezing along in the air sign of Gemini up until the 22nd. This is the area of your chart devoted to home and family. This is no bad thing because it's likely that these areas may have been neglected of late, but now you are being pointed in their direction and no matter how muddled or confused situations may be, you do have the confidence to find solutions. All you have to do is believe it.

From the 22nd onwards the Sun will be moving into the water sign of Cancer, and so you begin an enjoyable period of the year when you are flirty, sociable and in tiptop health. Try not to agonize over new relationships, greet them with an open mind and wait and see what will develop rather than trying to force the pace.

That quicksilver planet, Mercury, will be situated in

Cancer between the 7th and 27th, and because of this you may be drawn to intellectual pastimes rather than physical sport. Changes may take place in your social life, and someone may be introducing you to something which you find positively riveting.

Venus enters Leo on the 6th, throwing a rosy glow over your relationships with workmates as well as bringing a more hopeful feel to solving a professional problem. Do watch out for overindulgence though because Venus will be encouraging your sweet tooth as well as your liking for alcohol. You don't want to spend the entire month suffering from either a raging headache or an upset tummy do you?

Mars will be sailing along in the air sign of Libra throughout June, and because of this the emphasis on people you are financially dependent upon continues. It may be that such individuals are suffering from a good deal of stress and if you sense this to be the case, then see what you can do to ease the pressure, or at least give them your 100 per cent cooperation.

Now look at the *Daily Guides* for further information.

TUESDAY 1st Today's stars suggest that no matter how upset or hard done by you may feel at the moment, do try hard to count your blessings and remember what has been accomplished so far. Make the most of what is available to you at the moment and remember that no one can separate you from those you care about, undermine your confidence or stop you from realizing your goal once you have decided exactly what it is.

WEDNESDAY 2nd There could be a considerable

amount of upheaval where money is concerned. This may mean that you are raiding the shops – I fear that this is likely. Certainly, if this is the case, you will spend far more than you intended and it might be a better idea to send somebody else to do the shopping. Romantically, though, things look very promising and new people who enter your life will be stimulating and refreshing.

THURSDAY 3rd Whether you see today's stars as positive or negative will depend on your own attitude and awareness, but no one could accuse you of not having good reasons to get tough with those who have been taking your support and goodwill for granted. However, with many new areas to be explored, the question you must ask yourself is, are they worth the trouble?

FRIDAY 4th Finally, today, Mars resumes direct movement. This will make life considerably easier on the work front where matters and colleagues will be far less stressed out and complex than they have been of late. You'll have plenty of energy which will be equal to any task, all you have to do is believe it and then you'll be able to show other people just how ambitious and competent you really are.

SATURDAY 5th You will be much more light-hearted than you usually are, possibly because you are consumed by a flirty mood. If so, you can be quite sure that those around will be noticing in no uncertain fashion. There's a possibility, too, that you may be preparing for a special occasion and you'll whizz through what needs to be done in an efficient manner.

SUNDAY 6th Venus will be moving into the fiery sign of Leo, which is the area of your chart devoted to the daily grind. Certainly, where work matters are concerned you will be feeling far more confident as well as finding that other people are only too willing to do whatever they can to back you. You'll be mixing business with pleasure a great deal more than is usually the case and some of you may even be finding romance at work.

MONDAY 7th Mercury moves into the watery sign of Cancer and because of this, when it comes to socializing and having fun, you may be drawn to intellectual rather than frivolous pursuits. Should somebody wish to teach you backgammon, chess or something similar, why not try it, you're likely to find it fascinating as well as enjoyable.

TUESDAY 8th If you have an arrangement with friends, then you need to double-check that they know exactly where they are supposed to be and at what time. There could be some kind of muddle under this day's influences. Keep a civil tongue in your head, too, as there will be a strong temptation to give somebody a 'ticking off'.

WEDNESDAY 9th There seems to be a particular stress on communication, therefore if you are visiting other people, you have chosen well. If you are at home this evening, then you can expect the doorbell and telephone to be constantly ringing, and this makes you feel wanted and desired, which is just what you need right now.

THURSDAY 10th   At some point today you really must make an effort to escape from your usual surroundings and get out into the fresh air. You need some time to gather your wits and also to recover from a certain amount of exhaustion which you are likely to be suffering. A bit of deep breathing and a clean atmosphere will help to restore your spirits in record time.

FRIDAY 11th   Keep life running along well-oiled wheels today as this seems to be the best way to travel. Even though there are many options open to you, no one could blame you for wanting it all. Personally, financially, even emotionally, you have plenty to be happy about. There is a danger, however, that you could waste your chances. Above all, don't take on any new responsibilities until you've had time to think about them.

SATURDAY 12th   The day begins slowly, but seems to gather momentum as the hours pass. You may wake up feeling decidedly dissatisfied with life, but wait a while because your mood will change quite dramatically. The phone is likely to be red hot with invitations for the future, so get out your diary!

SUNDAY 13th   Today is the day of the New Moon and it occurs in the family and property areas of life. There may be some important news or an announcement which could surprise and delight some of you. For others, guests may turn up completely out of the blue and find a warm welcome.

MONDAY 14th This could be an affectionate and heart-warming day because you're at your most sympathetic and others will be responding in kind. Don't hold back on your thoughts and feelings as this is no time to be reserved or shy. The more you are ready to give out to other people, the more responsive they will be to you.

TUESDAY 15th Over the next couple of days or so money will come in from unusual people or unusual sources, so it would be a good idea to be much more adventurous. Open up your head to ideas you would normally dismiss as outrageous. It is certainly a good time, too, for minor changes at the work front.

WEDNESDAY 16th The Sun is in a beautiful aspect with Mars, therefore if you need to make any move connected with money, you can do so in the knowledge that you are doing the right thing at the right time. Money spent on entertaining this evening will be well worth it, and all in all this is a good positive day.

THURSDAY 17th If you have been feeling down recently, you will have good reason today to feel much more hopeful about the future. Perhaps a letter or phone call will do wonders for your morale. You should get out this evening and spend a modest amount on having fun.

FRIDAY 18th You should take even greater care than

usual when dealing with money or business matters. Simply refuse to be pushed into anything that you are not happy or comfortable with. Right now the line between your own thoughts and reality will become more than just a little blurred, so be cautious, otherwise you risk becoming entangled in the world of half-truths and confusion.

SATURDAY 19th Today the stars could make you more headstrong than is usually the case and you will want to lead from the front, even solve other people's problems for them. While no effort will be too much for you today, make certain that those receiving help are truly deserving of it.

SUNDAY 20th It's likely that your main objective today will be your status and standing at work. In fact, today's planetary setup suggests that the obstacles that have been blocking your way or thwarting your innermost ambitions will be swept to one side, never to return.

MONDAY 21st New faces and places have no doubt been giving you a difficult slant on life recently, but your real duties now lie much closer to home. Above all, your honesty, integrity and talent for putting others at their ease certainly will be in demand. This is an excellent evening for entertaining at home.

TUESDAY 22nd Today the Sun will be moving into the watery sign of Cancer, which is the area of your chart that represents sports, children, pleasure seeking and love. Luckily, you are in just the right mood to take advantage of the lighter-hearted atmosphere which prevails and will be a boon to any company that you attend. However, don't take your emotional reactions to members of the opposite sex too seriously otherwise you will have cause to regret it.

WEDNESDAY 23rd As a Fish, you are usually at your most content and happy in familiar surroundings with people you can count on and trust. The stars today certainly seem to indicate that your heart will be with trusted and true friends rather than acquaintances. A harsh word from an acquaintance will reinforce your determination to close ranks on the family front.

THURSDAY 24th People's tempers will be frayed, particularly those who are closest to you, therefore don't attempt to push your point home too strongly. Instead, open the lines of communication and listen to what they have to say. On a personal level, a physical attraction could spring up, but don't kid yourself that it is anything more than that.

FRIDAY 25th The starry setup will be letting you know whether or not you are on the right track as far as a creative project or an affair of the heart is concerned. If you should reach the decision that you are not, then don't be afraid to turn back and start again. Unless it is right from the beginning it is bound to be wrong in the end.

SATURDAY 26th Mercury today is in a difficult aspect with Jupiter, which simply means that those people closest to you are being too optimistic about a matter that is close to their heart. See if you can introduce a certain amount of common sense into their thinking, because like it or not you will be doing them a big favour.

SUNDAY 27th   The stars suggest that you try to remain on friendly terms with relatives and work colleagues. On no account try to force the pace, or spring any sort of surprise. It is a time for putting other people's wants and needs before your own. You'll find this relatively easy to do when in the right mood, which hopefully will descend today.

MONDAY 28th   Today is the day of the Full Moon and it occurs in the gritty sign of Capricorn. This represents the area of your chart devoted to friends and acquaintances, therefore there could be a falling out if you make excessive demands. Instead, see what you can do to support them for a change and then nothing untoward should occur.

TUESDAY 29th   If ever there was a time for sorting out family or work differences, this is most definitely it. If there are disagreements between yourself and a workmate or family member, then sit down and calmly sort out the problem. You may find in the end that you are not as far apart as you think you are.

WEDNESDAY 30th   The Sun is in a difficult aspect with Pluto, and because of this you may find a work colleague disruptive and frustrating. The thing for you to do, Pisces, is to keep yourself to yourself, which you are good at, get on with what concerns you and leave them to stew in their own juice for the time being, unless they ask for help, which is unlikely.

JULY

The Sun this month will be sailing along in the water sign of Cancer up until the 22nd. This is good news because it throws the focus on to creativity, which you're usually good at, romance, which you're usually preoccupied with, and also children if you happen to be a family person. There seems to a great deal of fun waiting for you and all you have to do is to get out into the big, wide world and make the most of what the stars hold for you.

From the 23rd onwards the Sun will be moving into the fiery sign of Leo, placing the emphasis on sheer hard work which is probably a result of matters you have overlooked due to your propensity for enjoyment early month. However, it's likely you will decide the price was worth paying for.

Mercury is in retrograde movement in the fire sign of Leo. A warning then that you will exhaust far more easily than is usually the case and so you must set aside time for rest and relaxation if you are not to end up feeling like a well-worn dishcloth. The choice is yours.

Venus will be coasting along in Virgo from the 13th onwards, increasing your chances for attending parties and meeting new people, which could very well lead to casual romance. However, don't take the latter too seriously, just be prepared to wait and see for a change. All too often members of your sign imagine they are in love when really they are in lust.

Mars continues its weary path through the water sign of Scorpio, therefore the tendency for you to fall out with people who come from very different backgrounds from yourself continues, which is very un-Piscean like. See what you can do to be as patient as you can with such individuals because before you know it you will either have formed a deep friendship or perhaps something even more important.

Now look at the *Daily Guides* for further information.

THURSDAY 1st   The stars today should give you every chance to have your say, especially at work or where a business matter is concerned. This aside, there is quite likely to be a situation which will stir up old rivalries if you allow this to occur. This is a fine time for taking the reins of control into your own hands and saying 'no more'.

FRIDAY 2nd   The planetary setup will be stirring up the adventurous side to your character. Just for once you are not happy to potter around at work or at home, but will want to visit those who live at a distance from you, and travelling should be smooth as well as enjoyable, with a nice warm welcome at the end of the day.

SATURDAY 3rd   You're beginning to understand where you are going and what you want. This process is an important step forward, and will help your emotional life considerably. Whatever else will be going on, you are now faced with the challenge of changing the old order and being responsible for your life, which you have found impossible up until now. The danger is that you will go forward too quickly and neglect important details or underestimate somebody who is far more powerful than you.

SUNDAY 4th   You have been waiting for some time to make your mark and now the time is approaching you feel less confident. There are obstacles to negotiate and discussions to finalize, but the planets are giving you a shove in the right direction. So get rid of those uncertainties and you will sail over the first fence. Some of that work will bring luck and will encourage you to see everything from a different perspective. In love you can't count on good fortune, but nothing stays the same for ever. So be compassionate and you will get there eventually.

MONDAY 5th   Mars will be moving into the watery sign of Scorpio, which is the area of your chart devoted to children, sports and casual romance. You'll certainly have added energy for anything physical, but you must make sure that you don't overdo it or strains and sprains could occur. Remember, too, that when you think you are in love you're probably in lust and should behave accordingly, so don't take anything which happens too seriously.

TUESDAY 6th   Despite some discontent and ill feeling in the friendship area of your chart, you seem to have your life very much under control. In fact, compared with a certain period earlier in the year, things look positively marvellous. But much of this has resulted from a change of attitude and a willingness to be more flexible. You're finding out that if you hold on to people and situations too tightly you are almost bound to lose them.

WEDNESDAY 7th   Life has rarely been quite as satisfactory as it is now and though you should keep a conservative eye on the future, don't deny yourself or your loved ones a little indulgence right now. Your life seems to be changing in a big way. Significant events or developments may not surface just yet, but the seeds are being sown for greater offensives later in the year. This isn't the time to capitalize on all that has been offered. Alter your outlook and expect things to be moving in a big way.

THURSDAY 8th   The series of events set in motion quite recently are reaching a conclusion. Financially or professionally – possibly both – you have no alternative but to resolve the issues. If nothing else, you will be glad that the whole story is finally at an end. But could it be that the consequences of your actions are nowhere near as bad as you once feared they might be?

FRIDAY 9th   If there are heavyweight jobs for you to perform, either at work or at home, then now is the time to get to grips with them. The planetary setup today will give you the energy, enthusiasm and staying power you need to get the job done. However, be sure to spell out exactly what is expected of loved ones, otherwise the day could end on a sour note.

SATURDAY 10th Your determination to succeed is quite unbelievable at present, but you are not alone – even though you probably think you are. Providing you can take a few minutes to ask, you will find that friends and acquaintances are ready to rally round and help you out in any way. An older person will be handing down some worthwhile advice, so don't allow that perverse streak of yours to strike you deaf as well as dumb. Their words are certainly worth listening to.

SUNDAY 11th Don't be surprised if the stars are pointing you towards a direction you would not normally be inclined to take. Yours, of course, is a water sign and one that possesses many great wishes. However, you will do well at some stage today and may discover something, I believe, a theory or philosophy, that answers many of the important questions you have been asking.

MONDAY 12th Mercury goes into retrograde action and because of this you will discover that it's much harder to pin other people down than is usually the case. Possibly, they're going through a period of indecision themselves, and they won't thank you for applying the pressure, so see what you can do to leave them alone for however long they deem necessary.

TUESDAY 13th Today is the day of the New Moon and it occurs in the watery sign of Cancer. For many of you there may be a new romance or perhaps an exciting social invitation. Either way, always remember that New Moons are an excellent time for making fresh starts and this one is no exception.

WEDNESDAY 14th Venus will be moving into your opposite sign of Virgo, which is good news because it throws a rosy glow over cooperation between yourself and other people. Should you be fancy-free, then during the ensuing week you'll be meeting several attractive people and one may just prove to be 'the one', so make sure you are looking good and circulate as much as you possibly can. After all, they're not going to come knocking at your door.

THURSDAY 15th Today it's likely you will become more contemplative, but don't lock yourself away from the rest of us. After all, if you use others as a sounding board, it may help you to decide what and who is important to you, and therefore the way ahead will be clearly signposted.

FRIDAY 16th You may suspect that someone is being anything but straightforward with you. If this is so, this would be the right time for a confrontation. However, make sure you remain calm, logical and fair-minded. It is a good time, too, for finding an outlet for one of your pet inspirations, because you will find other people extremely receptive to you right now. This evening, give time to that special someone in your life.

SATURDAY 17th There's likely to be a stop/go feel about the day that you may find frustrating. It's rather like holding a red rag in front of a bull, and we all know what happens next. Yes, it's very much a case of head down and charge ahead, trampling everyone and everything under foot. Try to control that frustration or apologies may become necessary at a later date.

SUNDAY 18th Should you want to make any social arrangements, then do so during the earlier part of the day. This is when you will find it easier to get hold of other people. Later on they may be elusive or simply too busy to talk to you. It might be a good idea to get into a mood of relaxation this evening, as you could end the day feeling shattered.

MONDAY 19th Today you become softer, more emotional and ready to take accept any changes that loved ones or colleagues put before you. You suddenly become more sociable, too, and whilst you're in a social whirl you will discover you seem to have many admirers. Yes, you can take your pick, what a lovely position to be in.

TUESDAY 20th It is other people who seem to be taking control, but just for once you don't seem to mind as you believe they know what they are doing and saying. There's a strong theme of change about the day, too, therefore take your adaptability to the drycleaners and prepare yourself for literally anything. It sounds an exciting time to me.

WEDNESDAY 21st You are reluctant to allow other people into your secret thoughts and plans. Not surprisingly then, loved ones may feel as if they are being permanently locked out or isolated and they could complain in no uncertain fashion. Make a positive effort to reach out to others into life because too much time spent alone will only lead to brooding, and this is a negative quality we can all do without.

THURSDAY 22nd   The stars today are certainly gingering up the family in no uncertain fashion. Everyone seems to be tearing around, but somebody needs to organize them, and quite frankly it might as well be you. Some of the excitement may have been caused by news about a member of the family – perhaps an engagement, a marriage or even a birth. Whatever it is, you can be sure that as far as families are concerned you are not going to be bored.

FRIDAY 23rd   The Sun will be moving into the fiery sign of Leo, which is the area of your chart that emphasizes workmates, hard slog and health. Quite clearly there may be a tendency for you to overdo it during the next few weeks or so and should this be the case, then you will be paying a high price. Slow yourself down, enjoy the scenery, because you won't know what you are missing, and it could be a great deal.

SATURDAY 24th   Wouldn't it be nice to think that everyone was now working towards the same goal? But the planets suggest that this is a rather naive way to think. The fact is you can't afford to take what others do or say at face value, especially at work. Be wary of those who offer advice before you have asked for it, because it may be that you have something they are after.

SUNDAY 25th   Although you have no intention of getting involved in some kind of partnership or emotional disagreement, others will still try to drag you in and force you to take sides. Tell family and friends that you have no particular sympathies one way or the other, even if it's not strictly true. It's important that you detach yourself from this. Later on, the chances are that it will be up to you to negotiate a compromise that leaves both sides happy – a difficult job.

MONDAY 26th The Sun is lining up in a difficult aspect with your ruling planet, Neptune, because of this you could be overconfident about an important matter, or act impulsively without sufficient planning. Before you rush out into life stop and pause if only for a moment and ask yourself: are you going in the right direction and with the right person? Unless you're sure about this it might be a good idea to stay where you are for the time being.

TUESDAY 27th The Sun today is in a difficult aspect with Jupiter, so your judgement may not be spot on where important work decisions are concerned and because of this it might be a good idea to discuss them with other people. You may make a fool of yourself if you don't and that's something you are sure to regret.

WEDNESDAY 28th Today is the day of the Full Moon and it occurs in a rather unsettling part of your chart. Therefore, you may lose confidence, feel unsure and maybe even unloved. Do try to remember that this is only your imagination firing on all cylinders and that you should not take your reactions to situations too seriously. Mind you, Full Moons can always be used for putting the finishing touches to any kind of project or work.

THURSDAY 29th   The stars today put you in a soft sentimental and nostalgic mood. However, this is perhaps not the ideal state to be in when dealing with competitors and rivals as it would be all too easy to take advantage of you. Therefore, save this soft mood for your family or that special someone in your life this evening.

FRIDAY 30th   The emphasis is on your natural characteristics and so this could lead you to become lazy and self-indulgent. But too little exercise and too much pleasure could ruin your health. The planetary setup today means it's just the time to begin a new health regime or visit a health club a little more frequently. Professionally, if you work as a member of a team, you should be getting results.

SATURDAY 31st   This is a time for pushing ahead with self-interests, whether emotional, professional or financial. Others are drawn to your magnetism and charm at present. It's a great time, too, for a special occasion or for the formation of a professional partnership. Your social life blossoms and you may be involved in taking a short break in the near future.

AUGUST

The Sun will be coasting along in the fiery sign of Leo up until the 23rd, so like it or not Pisces, it's hard work which seems to be dominating. Don't be tempted to take short cuts because you'll only need to redo everything all over again, which would be a pity. There's a chance, too, that you'll be getting on far better with workmates than is usually the case and probably socializing with them.

From the 23rd onwards the Sun will be moving into your opposite sign of Virgo, throwing the emphasis on a need to cooperate with other people as well as the formation of partnerships, both personal and professional. As a Fish, you hate to travel alone and during this period there is no reason for you to do so, not even for a moment.

Mercury will be moving into Leo on the 11th, bringing minor changes in the lives of your workmates as well as at work itself. If you have a chance to travel for the sake of professional matters, then snap it up because it's bound to be lucky for you.

Venus' retrograde movement will take it back into Leo on the 16th. This is a sure indication that you may be thinking of becoming involved with a colleague, workmate or contact. Try to resist this temptation because the affair is likely to be disappointing as well as unduly complicated and quite frankly you don't need either.

Mars will be coasting along in Scorpio all month, therefore if you are a student and attempting to study there will be a tendency for you to try and do too much all at the same time. Streamline your activities and then you'll make more progress than you could have hoped for.

Now look at the *Daily Guides* for further information.

SUNDAY 1st The Moon in your sign today indicates that this could be an extremely heartwarming and encouraging day. Even other people who perhaps have constantly opposed you in the past will now be running around doing what they can to make your life easier and a lot more fun too. Certainly, you have much more to look forward to than you have to fear.

MONDAY 2nd   The stars today are certainly gingering up your close relationships. There are likely to be new people entering your life, and minor changes and lots of news in connection with that special person. On the other hand, should you be alone, then this is a time for turning acquaintances into friends and friends into lovers. Someone close may be coming up with a money-making idea.

TUESDAY 3rd   You may be considering seriously some kind of domestic move or professional upheaval, but this is not an ideal time for any kind of action. You don't want to upset the status quo, or reject the past too quickly, therefore keep your thoughts to yourself for the time being. The stars today urge you to take as much time as you need to consider what a major change in your life would mean. If you move too fast too soon, then all you will do is swap one set of problems for another.

WEDNESDAY 4th   Travel seems to be very much on your mind even though most of it seems to be taking place inside your head. What you imagine today, you may achieve at a later date. No matter how far-fetched your ideas or your fancies, cling on to them, because eventually you will get the chance to turn dreams into a reality.

THURSDAY 5th   It seems today there is little time for

pleasantries or niceties, particularly where family or cash matters are concerned. If you have something important to say – no matter how distressing or painful – then you must speak out. You may not like having to take others to task, or pointing at the folly of their ways, but the situation will only get worse if you continue to ignore the evidence.

FRIDAY 6th Today will be gingering up those intensely personal relationships of yours. You may find others a little touchy and impulsive, but they are more physically aware, energetic and definitely sexy. Don't be surprised then if you find yourself being hotly pursued by the person you care about most. This, I think, qualifies the period as a good one – don't you?

SATURDAY 7th Mars is in a difficult aspect with Uranus, and so you must be careful of unexpected or sudden financial opportunities. If you dash ahead without due thought, I'm afraid you're going to regret it at a later date and probably in a big way too.

SUNDAY 8th This is the time to pussyfoot around, rather than to be too assertive. If you are, you will only upset other people, particularly where your social and professional ambitions are concerned. Should you be at work, then listen to what colleagues have to say and try your best not to offend people by being too direct. There's a time for being pushy and asserting your authority, but this is not one of them.

MONDAY 9th The stars are likely to stir up affairs

on the home front. Warring factions may explode, but having done so the lines of communication will be far more open once the dust has settled and a closer bond will have been formed.

TUESDAY 10th   There is a possibility of news reaching you by phone or letter from someone who lives quite a distance from home. It is likely, too, that a member of the family may do something which will take you back to the past in some way, and this results in a couple of quiet hours.

WEDNESDAY 11th   Today is the day of the New Moon and it falls in the fiery sign of Leo, this is the area of your chart devoted to routine work as well as colleagues, therefore you could either be starting a new relationship, which brings a better understanding, or possibly you are involved in trying to get a new project off the ground. Whichever applies, this is going to be a lucky day, so don't hesitate to push ahead with your dreams and wishes no matter what they may be.

THURSDAY 12th   Mercury will be moving into the fiery sign of Leo, and this will bring in plenty of news and change in the lives of your workmates and contacts. However, healthwise, you may become a little nervy during the ensuing days and it is important that you get sufficient rest to offset any possible problems.

FRIDAY 13th   Today's aspects certainly soften up people in positions of power or authority. So, shrink not from visiting the bank manager, tax collector or bureaucrats. All you need to do is to turn on that Piscean charm, which few can resist no matter what they do for a living.

SATURDAY 14th Your love of beauty and colour, and in fact all of your senses, are enhanced at this moment which some of you can put to practical use. For others, you are perhaps in a sentimental and romantic mood and this proves to be attractive to somebody else. Don't be surprised if you suddenly find yourself surrounded by admirers – lucky you.

SUNDAY 15th It looks as if somebody is going to be in the money and it is likely to be you. But make sure there isn't a catch before making a commitment. It seems almost too good to be true.

MONDAY 16th Venus's retrograde action may have an adverse affect on your love life. Your judgement may be completely off when it comes to gauging what other people feel about you, which is most unusual, but even you can step out of character from time to time and this seems to be one of those occasions.

TUESDAY 17th There seems to be a coming together between yourself and other people. Those who were once competitors turn out to be close friends. Likewise, somebody you thought of only as a friend turns out to be something rather special on the emotional or even sexual front. If you are in a steady relationship, then this is a time for kissing and making up if there have been any problems between you of late.

WEDNESDAY 18th Pluto goes into direct movement,

and because of this complications and difficulties which may have blocked your progress in connection with long-distance travelling, or perhaps education, slowly begin to melt away and you feel much more optimistic and go-getting. If you're expecting to hear from someone who lives at a distance, then they are likely to get in touch today.

THURSDAY 19th From hereon in it will pay you to cooperate and support, rather than insist on having everything your own way. This is certainly a great time for those who are thinking of forming relationships. The more you give to other people over the next few weeks the more you will get back, and not only in terms of money but also love and affection.

FRIDAY 20th Current aspects suggest that loved ones, as well as relatives, must be handled with a great deal of care during this particular day, otherwise you could run the risk of creating tension and resentment. Luckily, it appears that you seem to know exactly when to be quiet and when to make your feelings known. In fact, relationships in general are due to take a turn for the better over the next few days or so.

SATURDAY 21st As a Piscean, you have the reputation of being a defender of those who are helpless. However, many who fall under your sign possess a remarkably sharp tongue and their verbal tirades today can be all the more effective for being totally unexpected. So the planets urge you to remind those around you that however much you fight for them your efforts must not be taken for granted.

SUNDAY 22nd Today's stars suggest that you are coming to accept that some kind of emotional or personal change is unavoidable, as well as learning to be more realistic about family and cash expectations. Other people's motives have always seemed to be something of a mystery. Too often in the past you have judged those you loved and admired by standards that have been unrealistic. Now, at last, you're beginning to accept others as they really are.

MONDAY 23rd If you happen to be at work, then it's a good day for drawing attention to your talents and gifts. If you are not, then you are sure to find it difficult to turn off your drive and this may be somewhat irritating to those loved ones of yours. Why not get it over and done with and meet up with a colleague for an hour or so?

TUESDAY 24th At work, ambitions and colleagues seem to be on your mind. If you're not careful, loved ones are going to be grumbling and accusing you of neglecting them – and quite right too. There's a time and a place for everything and this is a day for your personal life rather than for the professional. Make a phone call by all means, but after that forget about it.

WEDNESDAY 25th You may be mystified about a professional problem, so get on the phone to others because they may be able to shed some light on this particular problem. This evening is a great time for teamwork, particularly if it is connected with sports. Youngsters will enjoy themselves when visiting clubs.

THURSDAY 26th   Today is the day of the Full Moon and it occurs in your own sign. Oh dear! You mustn't allow yourself to be dragged down by the influence of this planet, the trouble is that it tends to heighten your imagination and blow molehills into mountains. However, now you are aware of this fact perhaps you can do something constructive about it and don't use it as an excuse to wallow in self-pity.

FRIDAY 27th   There may be a certain amount of friction over a friendship today, so be careful what you say. Try hard to control your emotions and don't react to provocation. Tact is likely to be your best weapon in this direction. Creatively, at the moment there are no limits. Emotionally, you may be inclined to read into situations more than really exists because that imagination of yours is firing on all cylinders.

SATURDAY 28th   The Moon is, of course, an ever-changing planet and it has entered your sign. Because of this it will seem to you that there is no opening for direct action concerning one situation which is irritating you tremendously. Whatever you do, don't force change too soon or overreact to those around. This is a time for pulling in the reins, for slowing down and enjoying the scenery. If you're trying to get from place to place, you may find your journey disrupted.

SUNDAY 29th   Your boss may be screaming and his

secretary may be in tears, but you seem to be impervious. It's very much a case of head down and battle on until you have finished what you started. This evening it is likely that you are adopting a more serious attitude to your emotions, and many of you may be thinking about the long-term future in a way that you would not have thought possible a couple of weeks ago.

MONDAY 30th   You're always anxious and insistent to ensure that other people know exactly where you stand and what you think. You know your views are important and indeed they are, but you may not say precisely what you mean when speaking in haste. Unless you are careful this could be an accident-prone day, so go cautiously.

TUESDAY 31st   It may be a good idea to adopt a more cynical attitude towards yourself today. You will be changing your mood on the hour, every hour of the day. Confused? How do you think other people feel? Because of this mood it might not be a good idea to commit yourself to anything which requires intense concentration. Busy yourself with putting the finishing touches to already started jobs or chores.

SEPTEMBER

The Sun this month will be coasting along in your opposite sign of Virgo up until the 22nd. Fortunately, you are one sign who doesn't always insist on having your own way, which is just as well because you will need to consider other people and much more for the time being.

After the 22nd, the Sun will be moving into the air sign of Libra, which is the area of your chart devoted to people you are financially dependent upon. It looks as if they could certainly do with some encouragement from you, so see what you can do.

Mercury, too, will be coasting along in Virgo until the 17th, so new people will be entering your life and livening it up a great deal. This applies to all areas, romantic as well as professional.

Venus will be sparkling away in the fiery sign of Leo, and this will certainly be throwing a rosy glow over your relationships with workmates. Even those uncongenial jobs can be tackled without any moans and groans from you – for a change. Some of you may even be becoming romantically involved with workmates and as long as they are being honest with you, then why not?

Mars will be drifting along at the zenith of your chart from the 3rd onwards, suggesting that a lot of good hard work will be done. Although you may complain of this from time to time, you'll be feeling very satisfied with yourself at a later date if you stick at it. However, it is important that you rest and relax otherwise you won't be able to cope, well, only with a great deal of difficulty I can assure you.

Now look at the *Daily Guides* for further information.

WEDNESDAY 1st   It's quite likely that life on the home front has been anything but congenial, and probably downright upsetting and unnerving. If this should be the case, then it is more important than ever to find common ground now on which you can build bridges. You will need to find points of agreement before relationships can blossom again. This may apply to other sides to life too.

THURSDAY 2nd Certainly if you work in big businesses, such as a banking, insurance or even government bodies, then you can make a fresh start in some way. For all Pisceans, now is the time for widening your horizons and being your usual ambitious self.

FRIDAY 3rd Mars will be moving into the fiery sign of Sagittarius and this is the zenith point of your chart, and so you can expect to work a good deal harder for your money than is usually the case. Failure to do so is likely to lead to a dip in popularity which, of course, you won't want – now, will you?

SATURDAY 4th Many of you may be making a new start or perhaps enrolling in a fresh course of learning. Foreign affairs and long-distance travel will also be highlighted over the next few days or so. It's certainly going to be an interesting period.

SUNDAY 5th The stars today seem to produce a stop/go feel about the day. Naturally, you may find interruptions to your progress somewhat frustrating, and it will be all you can do to remain your normal calm, serene and, of course, charming self. Best not to argue with superiors, no matter what the provocation.

MONDAY 6th Uranus is in aspect to the Sun and

because of this your progress at work may be somewhat patchy, mind you, you don't seem to have a great deal of energy at your disposal, so perhaps this is just as well. Plan a relaxing time this evening where you can really put your feet up and let the troubles of the world disappear.

TUESDAY 7th   It's likely that you've been racing around far too much recently. It is now important that you find some way of sorting out arguments and disagreements as well as looking at ways of getting more support from everyone concerned. If you are still bearing grudges where a mate is concerned, then forget it. This goes against the grain anyway and so should be easy to let go. Relax and think of future gains.

WEDNESDAY 8th   The stars put you in the mood for making changes. This could surprise a few people when you start things new or bring other things to a happy conclusion. You're able to sort out family and property matters, too, because you have greater confidence in these areas. Don't be afraid to make a few waves.

THURSDAY 9th   Today is the day of the New Moon and it occurs in the fiery sign of Sagittarius. This is the zenith point of your chart and so if you want to make any changes on a professional level, you've certainly got the green light from the stars. Somebody new enters your life in connection with your job, so make sure they receive a warm welcome as it's better to have them on your side than against you.

FRIDAY 10th   The Sun is lining up with Saturn, and

this will be increasing your concentration so that you can get through what needs to be done in record time. Perhaps the reason for your haste is because you have a special social occasion planned for this evening, which is a strong possibility, and if so then everything should go according to plan.

SATURDAY 11th Venus finally moves into direct movement, and so complications in your love life slowly begin to be a thing of the past. Creative work will shoot ahead in leaps and bounds, too, and you have a great deal to look forward to.

SUNDAY 12th This is a good time for those who want to study or who are perhaps already in the process of learning a new skill. A good time, too, for booking travel for the future as you should be able to find some kind of bargain. Interesting new strangers may enter your life this evening and a brief liaison is likely.

MONDAY 13th The stars will certainly be gingering up your grey matter, but when it comes to intricate work you may be a little bit in too much of a hurry and could overlook details. Retrace your steps in order to minimize future inconvenience when errors will be discovered.

TUESDAY 14th Mars and Pluto are in aspect today, and so for some of you there may be a strong attraction to a person who comes from a different background from your good self. Luckily, you are able to bridge any differences without any difficulty whatsoever. For others, there's a certain urgency about work and you'll need to get cracking, so no procrastinating please.

WEDNESDAY 15th Monies that are owed may finally roll in. Be quick to snap up any chances to improve the figures on your bank statements as they may not come again. Avoid spending money before it has actually had time to rest in your bank for more than a couple of hours.

THURSDAY 16th Other people may be putting pressure on you, but at least when you emerge you will be wiser and stronger as a result. Just be careful not to lose your sense of humour, that would not only be a loss to you, but also to the rest of us. You mustn't get overemotional, especially where cash is concerned, be sensible and you will have little to worry about.

FRIDAY 17th Mercury has moved into the sign of Libra, and so the emphasis seems to be on people you are financially dependent upon. It is likely that they are signing a new contract or perhaps leaving on a trip in connection with money, either way wish them 'good luck'. They'll be back before you've really had time to miss them anyway.

SATURDAY 18th You keep having patches when the level of nervous tension rockets, but calmer days are near, and you can afford to become less self-absorbed and much more outgoing. Begin making social arrangements but remember that the family want your company, too, as do your lovers – nice to be in demand.

SUNDAY 19th You future plans will go through periods

of intense upheaval today and almost everything you thought was fixed seems to be changing again. What you must do is find your bearings again and take time to reflect before you can push ahead with any commitment. Cast your mind back to a few days ago when you knew exactly what you wanted out of life and then you'll soon be able to get back on track once more.

MONDAY 20th   Ideally, you need to be with beautiful people and in beautiful places, although this could be difficult to achieve. Nevertheless, on the work front you'll find workmates in a congenial and helpful mood and this will help you through the day. This evening may have a nostalgic feel about it.

TUESDAY 21st   You have been going through a tense period of change and unpredictability. You must find a way of removing the uncertainty and the rather impulsive streak which has made you act so much out of character. There are more secure days ahead, of that you can be sure. Monies that were expected are likely to roll in, but the amount may not live up to your high expectations.

WEDNESDAY 22nd   You need to tread very carefully where the feelings of contacts, friends and acquaintances are concerned. One wrong word and they will be out the door. Luckily, your sign is one that is noted for its charm and you're going to need it today.

THURSDAY 23rd   The Sun will be moving into the air

sign of Libra, which is the area of your life devoted to people you are financially dependent upon. Luckily, this will put them in a good mood but they will be expecting something in return, but don't worry because all they are hoping for is a little bit of encouragement, so see what you can do.

FRIDAY 24th Friends, club activities and teamwork are emphasized. If you are single, it is likely that others will be making some interesting introductions. If you are a freelance worker, then get out and hustle like you have never hustled before.

SATURDAY 25th Today is the day of the Full Moon and it occurs in the fiery sign of Aries. This is the cash area of your life and so you need to hang on to your possessions, otherwise they could go missing which may upset you. Regardless of whether they are of monetary value or not, they have nostalgic value and you don't like to be parted from what is yours.

SUNDAY 26th From hereon in you need to be extremely careful when dealing with educational matters, travel or legal affairs. It will pay you to double-check and even treble-check as complications which occur in this area could be expensive in terms of time and money.

MONDAY 27th It's quite clear that the more effort you put into life the richer the rewards will be. There is a time, too, when minor changes at work may temporarily throw you, but they will work out in your favour, so get out your adaptability.

TUESDAY 28th You have been labouring for many days with a rather controlling influence and now is the time when you need to escape from this because you need more space. Make sure that you are not any more disruptive than it is necessary to be.

WEDNESDAY 29th There could be a way out of any cash problems if only you can hang on to your nerve. Partners, or other people in general, are in a highly unpredictable mood, so you must protect your own security first and ensure that you are not too dependent on them. Luckily, it is difficult to imagine you getting yourself into this state in the first place.

THURSDAY 30th You're always aware that you need a great deal of attention and you have not been getting enough recently. Not everything feels comfortable. The more you push, the more it feels that others are resisting you. Don't let jealousy interfere with one of your relationships, whether personal or professional.

OCTOBER

The Sun will be coasting along in Libra up until the 23rd, therefore the tendency for you to turn most of your attention to the affairs of work colleagues and work itself continues. You may not exactly be gaining the garlands at the moment but they will come in the not too distant future, so all you have to do is hang on.

From the 23rd onwards the Sun will be moving into the water sign of Scorpio. This has a direct bearing on further education, long-distance travel and foreigners. There's an exciting flavour about this period of the month and is likely to fill you with excitement.

Mercury will be moving into the water sign of Scorpio, bringing concentration to those of you who are studying and a certain amount of luck if you are taking any kind of test or examination. The Piscean who has friends abroad is likely to be hearing from them and will be delighted with what they are told.

Venus will be moving through your opposite sign of Virgo from the 8th onwards, and this throws a happy contented glow over all existing relationships, both at work and at home. If you are fancy-free, you should take a second look at any new face that enters your social scene, otherwise you may overlook someone who could mean a great deal to you, so take your head out of the clouds and be alert.

Mars will be moving into the earthy sign of Capricorn on the 17th, and because of this it is your male friends who are likely to be important. They may come to you for advice or, conversely, it may be you who is seeking some kind of support from them. Either way, you'll be getting closer with them and as a Piscean you love to know that others care about you, regardless of your sex.

Now look at the *Daily Guides* for further information.

FRIDAY 1st   The Sun is in a pleasant aspect with Pluto, and so you're feeling exciting and want to make plans for the future, and may even book a break for a couple of days. For others, it may be that you are hearing from somebody who lives at a distance and the fact they have got in touch delights you. You were beginning to think that perhaps they had forgotten your existence – it doesn't take much to make a Piscean feel insecure.

SATURDAY 2nd   You are running around in several circles, which is guaranteed to make you and other people feel dizzy. If you rush about like this and become too outspoken, the result could very well be that you ruffle the wrong feathers, so make sure you are being careful. This evening the stars suggest you spend time locally, perhaps popping in on friends or relatives who live close by.

SUNDAY 3rd   You begin a period when there's a strong possibility that you'll become romantically involved with those who live at a distance, maybe even foreigners. Certainly there's a happy glow over travel matters and foreign affairs for the next few weeks or so. If you have someone special abroad, then there's a good chance that they will be getting in touch with you today.

MONDAY 4th   It's perfectly true to say that in the main your courage and initiative usually pay off, but today you may find yourself in hot water because you were too impatient or overreacted. Just for once you can comfortably trust the advice of those around you who are more hard-headed than you are. Astrological activity in the home area of your chart seems to suggest you have guests this evening.

TUESDAY 5th   Mercury moves into the water sign of Scorpio today, and so if you have friends or contacts abroad, then they are certainly going to be in touch with you during the next couple of weeks or so. Those of you who are involved in higher education will find that grey matter firing on all cylinders and information will sink in a great deal easier than is usually the case.

WEDNESDAY 6th Mercury is in a difficult aspect with Neptune, and so you may become woolly-headed and absent minded. Better make sure that you don't take any treasured possessions out of your home, otherwise you'll spend a great deal of time looking for them and getting hotter and hotter under the collar. There's also a possibility of a disagreement between yourself and somebody else which could grow out of all proportion if you allow it to.

THURSDAY 7th You could be feeling about ready to blow your top – but is it wise? The stars suggest that the situation at home needs a certain amount of tact and tender loving care, and not sulking or tantrums. If you feel too wound up to discuss anything in a civil matter, then go quietly off by yourself and hold your tongue.

FRIDAY 8th Venus will be moving into the earthy sign of Virgo, throwing a rosy glow over all your closest relationships. However, if you happen to be fancy-free, then don't lose heart because there's a strong possibility that you may meet someone very special during the weeks that lie ahead. If you're already in a relationship, you may want to take it a step further and become engaged or even name the day.

SATURDAY 9th Today is the day of the New Moon

and it occurs in the airy sign of Libra. This suggests a new beginning for somebody you are financially dependent upon and, of course, this will indirectly rub off on you in the not too distant future. As always with New Moons, it's a time for adopting a fresh look, a new attitude or even going off in a completely different direction.

SUNDAY 10th There seem to be some amazing matters that are about to come to light, which you had either not known or had chosen to ignore because it suited you to do so. It may all seem highly unsettling at the moment, but in the long run you'll begin to feel very much more relieved. The stars suggest that you should be more adventurous in your social life this evening.

MONDAY 11th Explosions on the home front are likely unless you turn on that abundant charm of yours and keep warring factions well apart. It might be a good idea to take care around the house as minor mishaps may occur.

TUESDAY 12th There are likely to be some changes in your career, or the general direction of your life, and you might have wished for a slightly easier and calmer trip into these new times. Don't make matters worse by getting on your 'high horse' or crying buckets of tears because that would be just hurt pride.

WEDNESDAY 13th The stars seem to suggest that there are clashes between yourself and relatives, and all of you are being extremely stubborn. Somebody has got to give just a little and it might just as well be you Pisces, as you are the one with the soft heart. Come on, why not give it a whirl?

THURSDAY 14th A lively but practical mood has you ready for fun, games and flirtations. Whatever else happens right now, don't let yourself be pushed into a corner. Be ready to demand your moment of glory in the spotlight. After all, who can deny a Pisces this when most of the time you are content to take a back seat?

FRIDAY 15th This is likely to be an active and inter-esting day if you are at work, but if not, you may decide to protect yourself by disappearing into the home, family or a secluded niche somewhere. You don't want to be hassled or hustled through the day or the evening. Give yourself time on your own to think calmly. This isn't the time to get overwhelmed by too much advice, although plenty will be flying around.

SATURDAY 16th You are buzzing around at a rate of knots and are surrounded by friends and team-mates. You're very eager and enthusiastic to have your voice heard at the moment. This may not always be easy because you seem to be bamboozling others on occasions. Slow yourself right down if you want to make the best effect.

SUNDAY 17th Mars is in a beautiful aspect with Jupiter, making for a very lively day indeed. The more you keep on the go, the more enjoyable your time will be. This evening, make sure you get out and about and keep a very high profile because you will be attracting the opposite sex in droves.

MONDAY 18th Venus is in a difficult aspect with Pluto, and because of this you may find it difficult to travel from place to place without attracting snarl-ups and problems with your transportation. It might be a good idea to work out your route before you leave home and in that way you may be able to sidestep potential difficulty.

TUESDAY 19th You want more in the way of security, so you are working hard to clear mountains of paperwork and redoing your budget calculations. However, you are fickle enough to want to spend as well on things that make you feel pampered and sensuous, but this could be difficult to achieve. In fact, if you have managed to do so, write to me personally explaining your formula.

WEDNESDAY 20th If everybody else is preoccupied, then make sure you are giving yourself the permission to spoil yourself to a degree. Don't be too ready to leap in with offers of help or your energy will start to drain quickly. Too much work is already making you feel somewhat nervous and edgy.

THURSDAY 21st The Moon in your own sign is likely to make you hypersensitive and very indulgent. Make certain you get the right people around you for the best effect, because this is the time when you want to be seen. One friend or workmate is being quite critical, so you must be ready to be practical and detached with him/her and ignore any little pinpricks to that ego of yours.

FRIDAY 22nd   You may be feeling a little insecure but luckily friends will rally round and give you support and good advice. You'll want to be discussing your long-term future more effectively, and giving yourself a sensible game plan for the next few months or so. This evening is best spent catching up on the sleep that you have missed out on recently.

SATURDAY 23rd   The stars today are filling you with optimism, increasing your energy levels and waking up those hormones in a big way. Wherever you go, you will be drawing attention to yourself simply by being there, you don't have to do anything. It is a good time for asking for favours or presenting new ideas to other people, so don't hesitate to do so.

SUNDAY 24th   Today is the day of the Full Moon and it occurs in the earthy sign of Taurus. This suggests that you need to take care when moving from place to place, particularly if you are driving, and even if not, it might be a good idea to check timetables otherwise you could be hanging around for quite some time. If you're socializing this evening, it might be a good idea to get away from your neighbourhood and be a little bit more adventurous.

MONDAY 25th   Be prepared to go slightly out on a limb if it seems necessary because you very much want to be noticed. Giving in to others may be the best way of getting what you want, and besides, this is the talent you possess anyway. Your feelings will be more on display, but that isn't a bad thing for you.

TUESDAY 26th It's possible you are pleased to be out of what has been a rather stormy, bad-tempered and overwrought couple of days and so you could feel like celebrating. Your luck is about to turn for the better very shortly and you will soon find romance, friendship and more fun entering your life.

WEDNESDAY 27th Now, if you have to stand still for a while and dig down in order to get some sensible answers, then so be it. This is not a time for short cuts or easy solutions to problems, although no doubt you would prefer it to be. Letting go of the past may be one way of facing up to cash and emotional matters. Be sure you keep that temper of yours under control.

THURSDAY 28th With Venus in your opposite sign, the stars are certainly throwing a rosy and happy glow over all of your relationships, be they personal or professional. Those with whom you once argued and disagreed seem to be coming down in your favour. Social invitations are being given out by workmates, and it is a particularly useful day if you are involved in creativity of any description.

FRIDAY 29th There's suggestion here that over the next few days you may gain quite considerably through people in positions of authority, such as a tax collector or lawyer. During the next few days or so, think twice before splashing out on something unnecessary and merely decorative. You are attractive enough to light up any room, you don't need any extra glitz or glitter.

SATURDAY 30th It looks as though there is some unexpected expense, which quite frankly you don't need, in connection with home or family. You may whinge and grumble for a while, but being the warmhearted person you are you will eventually fork out, albeit reluctantly. Avoid expensive or extravagant pastimes.

SUNDAY 31st The stars suggest that relatives are in a rather fickle mood, so you know you need to tread very delicately and fit in with what will suit them just for once. Only by giving are you going to get the support you need in return. Avoid the temptation to shut yourself away behind a brick wall simply because you cannot get your own way, it would be self-defeating.

NOVEMBER

This month the Sun will be drifting along in the water sign of Scorpio up until the 22nd. This places the emphasis on foreign affairs, long-distance travelling and learning. If you're taking any kind of course, or perhaps simply want to improve your image, then this is the time to leap into action. Naturally, you probably want to look your best when the festive period arrives, which is not too far over the horizon.

From 23rd onwards the Sun will be moving into the zenith point of your chart into the fiery sign of Sagittarius.

Suddenly, you're consumed with an uncharacteristic urge to 'get ahead', which is all very well as long as you pace yourself otherwise you may suffer from strains and stresses. Those in positions of power or authority will be smiling sweetly down upon you, so if you need any kind of favour, this is the time to ask before it's too late.

Mercury will be drifting along in retrograde movement into Scorpio, so keep your mind on any kind of detailed work. You could drift off into one of those fantasies of yours and make some glaring mistakes which will no doubt be picked up by other people and probably to their delight.

Venus moves into Libra on the 9th, highlighting the affairs of people you are financially dependent upon. There seems to be some good luck for them which will, indirectly, rub off onto your good self. Emotionally, feelings will be running deeper and just for once you may be trying to develop one relationship rather than indulging in a crowd of admirers, which you now begin to realize produces precious little satisfaction.

Mars floats around in Capricorn up until the 26th, gingering up your intuition, but also leading to a certain amount of impatience with day-to-day detail. If you're not careful, you may overlook something which may have to be redone several times and this will try your patience to the limit. It would be best to sidestep this little pitfall in the first place if you possibly can.

Now look at the *Daily Guides* for further information.

MONDAY 1st It's likely that things will be somewhat frosty on the emotional front, although there is loyalty from a special person. Emotional disruptions pave the way for better relationships even though you may not realize it at this moment in time. Everyday routine is likely to be hectic, so hang on to your hat.

TUESDAY 2nd   Mercury is lining up with Neptune, and so there's a strong possibility that other people at work will perhaps be more creative and imaginative than your good self, for a change. Don't allow this to depress you in any way, shape or form, but simply pick up on their ideas and add your own brand of unique thought and you may find that you are on to a winner. Romantically, this is a day when you are likely to be drawing closer to other people and if you don't have anyone special in your life, well, then the stars may just be putting that right for you.

WEDNESDAY 3rd   You feel like speaking your mind when it comes to money matters, but be wary of leaping to conclusions and going off at a tangent. You need to be sensible when it comes to comes to cash. Luckily, the stars today suggest that there's plenty of practical ideas to back up your imagination, so your inspirations should take root. Be charming and diplomatic when you can at work.

THURSDAY 4th   The planetary setup today has your mind leaping ahead at a rate of knots. Other stars suggest you will feel in a challenging mood, but this may not be all that great an idea, especially on the home front. Don't feel you have to rock the boat or insist on an uncompromising stance. Try to see where steady effort can turn financial matters around to your advantage.

FRIDAY 5th The Sun is in a difficult aspect with Uranus, and so whether you are aware of it or not you may be feeling somewhat tense. It might not be a good idea to tackle anything of world-shattering importance right now, instead, be patient and wait for a more appropriate time.

SATURDAY 6th The Sun is in a difficult aspect with Saturn, therefore it's best not to socialize with workmates as they could be uptight and perhaps unreasonable. Stick to the same old crowd when seeking enjoyment this evening, because that's where you're most likely to find it.

SUNDAY 7th Although you know perfectly well that staying silent or listening as quietly as you can would be the best idea, you can hardly stop yourself leaping feet first into discussions. However, there are times when you just know that getting on with chores, dull though it sounds, is unavoidable. Find the balance between excitement and duty if you can.

MONDAY 8th Today is the day of the New Moon and it occurs in the watery sign of Scorpio. This is the area of your chart devoted to learning as well as foreign affairs, therefore, if you have anyone important abroad, you're sure to be hearing from them either by letter or phone. Any chance to get out this evening to new places should be snapped up at the speed of light.

TUESDAY 9th Venus will be moving into the air sign of Libra, and this throws a helpful glow over the financial affairs of other people who are closest to you. However, if they should experience a lucky break, do make sure that they don't spend their ill-gotten gains on too much celebrating otherwise they'll be back at square one before they know what has happened.

WEDNESDAY 10th   You are having quite brilliant inspirations and ideas which may point the way to new solutions to old financial problems. Some opportunities you need to run with instantly and some you need to double-check. The tricky question is deciding which falls into which category. Be sympathetic behind the scenes at home and the atmosphere will become more settled.

THURSDAY 11th   You need to walk your own road because it is strongly highlighted right now, so you are finding cooperation rather difficult. Just give yourself space at certain points in the day to follow your whims and then you will find the adjustments demanded by companions easier to accept at another time. You feel you are popular with friends and team mates.

FRIDAY 12th   Mercury is lining up in a difficult aspect with Jupiter, and because of this you will find other people, both at work and at home, are perhaps too optimistic in their assessment of situations. Of course, you can't blunder in and tell them so in a straightforward fashion, but if you pile on the compliments first and then point out the error of their ways you'll find them much more accepting.

SATURDAY 13th   The rumblings of discontent behind

the scenes or maybe a tense atmosphere is making you feel very edgy. Whatever occurs don't force yourself into saying more than you want to before the time is right. You need to keep smiling sweetly, sorting out your finances with charm rather than force. Ignore worries which will never come to pass.

SUNDAY 14th Friends are all over the place and pushing you into what you consider to be rather wild plans and schemes. Normally, you are imaginative and a touch adventurous but maybe you are just sitting back a little at the moment, taking everything with a large grain of salt. Stay cool but open-minded. Compliments from a distance will boost your morale and make you look ahead optimistically.

MONDAY 15th A love seems to be hidden, but there may be generous, although small, gestures from somebody who means a great deal to you which will please you. Make sure you are absolutely wide awake and alert at work. There are all sorts of possibilities ahead for very positive changes, but you need to be clear what is in your interests and what needs to be resisted.

TUESDAY 16th You know you really should be keeping your head down to sort out all kinds of rather picky details. However, in typical Piscean fashion, you would much rather be flying off after more entertaining prospects. If you feel the urge to disagree just for effect, grit your teeth and hold back. You have a mischievous, rebellious streak which can cause problems.

WEDNESDAY 17th You have a light-hearted humorous approach at the moment, though you are possibly more edgy than you will admit because of the planetary setup, which hints that you need to let go a little. Shine light on hidden places and be clear that letting go of the past is the only way ahead. Joint cash matters may be rather erratic, but there are gains to be made.

THURSDAY 18th Almost all of the energies at the moment are focusing your mind on home and relationship matters. Throw aside the old patterns and try to see where you can be more experimental in your approach. Clearly, you want love and affection, but you also need freedom and room to follow your own inclinations, but don't force a partner's hand this evening.

FRIDAY 19th You have a busy routine and are rather highly strung right now. Don't fly off the handle over trivia, or say too much in the heat of the moment. You may be right, but others may not take kindly to your pointing out their shortcomings. Luckily, the pleasant mood at home is keeping you on an even keel and money is slowly coming around.

SATURDAY 20th Venus is in a difficult aspect with Saturn, and because of this it wouldn't be a good idea to expect favours or advice from your friends, because it's likely that they have problems of their own. Don't fret, however, because it's likely that given a little space you can find your own solution.

SUNDAY 21st Venus is in a beautiful aspect with

Uranus, gingering up your imagination and your intuition. The only question is, Pisces, are you going to listen to it? I certainly hope so because it would be putting you on the right tracks and not only in your professional life but also in your personal life.

MONDAY 22nd The Sun moves into the fiery sign of Sagittarius, which is the zenith part of your chart and so from hereon in you'll be concentrating far more than is usually the case on your ambitions and getting ahead with work that has perhaps been left undone. Make sure, however, that you don't trample on other people's sensitivities as you push your way up the ladder of success.

TUESDAY 23rd Today is the day of the Full Moon and it occurs in the air sign of Gemini. It's likely then that there may be the end of a cycle in connection with property or family affairs. This should mean that recent tensions can now be swept to one side.

WEDNESDAY 24th There is no point in attempting to fathom other people out because just as you think you have reached some conclusion about them, they change yet again. It is best to allow them to follow their own erratic path for the time being while you follow yours. People you meet today could be useful as well as enjoyable company.

THURSDAY 25th You may be tackling matters which normally wouldn't bother you, for example, considering the possibility of taking out insurance policies or even confronting your bank manager. It is an excellent time for those who work in big business. However, it is a little quiet on the social front this evening.

FRIDAY 26th You will get about as far as you can in one particular direction and then have to retrace your steps before you can continue forward. Delays and frustrations might mean that someone else could temporarily get ahead of you. Never mind, your turn will come soon and you will be able to catch up in no uncertain fashion. This evening you may feel guilty about enjoying yourself, especially if you are being entertained by someone who is temporarily out of pocket.

SATURDAY 27th You can make important financial decisions today under favourable circumstances. You may also meet up with somebody who has an excellent financial suggestion, which you should at least be prepared to consider. When it comes to having fun today you are likely to opt for quieter pleasures because your nerves are beginning to jangle a bit, therefore be careful with whom you spend your time.

SUNDAY 28th You don't like misunderstandings arising in any area of your life, but you go to great lengths to avoid them cropping up in matters related to money or long-term security. The planets are in something of a grumpy mood so such caution is not only wise but crucial.

MONDAY 29th The stars seem to be suggesting today that decision time is coming closer, but don't let yourself be steamrolled into commitments of any description. It's not until a little later that you will be in a position to resolve the matters in question.

TUESDAY 30th It may be unsettling to have to change horses midstream, but don't turn down what arises suddenly just because you feel it could be inconvenient or disruptive. The starry setup today suggests that it is exactly what seems most inconvenient in the short term that could bring you the greatest long-term benefits.

DECEMBER

The Sun will be coasting along at the zenith of your chart up until the 21st, and so you are more than usually ambitious and have your head down attending to problems before they've even had a chance to arise. After the 22nd the Sun will be moving into the earthy sign of Capricorn, emphasizing the friendship and contact areas of your life. It's likely therefore that you'll be sorting out problems of those who are close to you as well as possibly meeting new people. Club activities will be well starred too.

Mercury will be coasting along at the zenith of your chart from the 11th onwards and if you are out of work, then this is an ideal time for going to any kind of meeting, audition or interview. For others already settled, minor changes can be instigated and it's quite likely that some of you may be signing an important document too.

Venus will be entering Scorpio on the 6th, throwing a happy glow over legal matters and foreign affairs. If you have someone special abroad, it's likely that they'll be getting in touch with you, or it may be that you are drawn to members of the opposite sex who come from abroad. Well, Pisces, you always did like something that was that little bit 'different'. However, don't jump in feet first because it's unlikely this relationship will last for any length of time.

Mars will continue to coast along in the air sign of Aquarius, gingering up your imagination and intuition. The question is, are your going to listen to your intuition instead of insisting on having all the facts and figures? Allow the dreamy side of your character to take over and go with the flow of events, then you're sure to find success in any area that you choose.

Now look at the *Daily Guides* for further information.

WEDNESDAY 1st You can't afford to let things go on without clarifying certain matters that involve some combination of money matters and friends or colleagues. You may have been putting off these exchanges in the hope that things would resolve themselves – in typical Piscean fashion. However, left unattended they could only get more complicated in the long run.

THURSDAY 2nd You may not be interested in any details concerning money just now, but the aspects today accent life's practicalities and this seems to be where your obligations and duty lie. On the plus side, any effort you make now is likely to be handsomely rewarded in the not too distant future, so why don't you just go for it.

FRIDAY 3rd The Sun is in a close aspect with Pluto, and because of this you may be feeling unsettled and with no clear reason as to why this should be. Imagination may be blocked too, therefore, if you are in an artistic job, I'm afraid there's likely to be a good deal of frustration on this particular day. What to do? Well, simply stick to routine, put the finishing touches to work and save major moves for the time being.

SATURDAY 4th The answer to overcoming difficulties, most of which have more to do with understanding than the issues themselves, is a gentle persistence, of which you have plenty. This may mean having to explain your thinking while going over the facts again and again, but if you can be patient, enlightenment will finally come to other people.

SUNDAY 5th Even the most tricky of misunderstandings in your personal life should give in to analysis of the situation. If you take time to delve deeper into certain matters beyond recent problems, you should be able to put matters to right. Experience, hopefully, will teach you how to prevent such difficulties cropping up again.

MONDAY 6th Venus will be moving into the watery sign of Scorpio, and because of this you may be strongly attracted to people who come from vastly different backgrounds from yourself, possibly from abroad. Maybe you're in one of your exotic moods, which is all very well as long as you don't allow the other person concerned to believe that you care for them more than you actually do.

TUESDAY 7th Today is the day of the New Moon and

it occurs in the zenith of your chart. You are provided then with an excellent time for making all-important professional moves, whether it be looking for a job, chasing promotion or simply winning over the opposition to your side.

WEDNESDAY 8th   Venus is in a difficult aspect with your ruler, Neptune, so you might be in a slapdash and careless frame of mind. The best thing for you to do is to stick to routine for the time being. But if you must work on something which requires creativity, then my advice to you is to go over it again and again, because each time you do you're sure to find that you have been mistaken or have made an error.

THURSDAY 9th   The Sun today is in a beautiful aspect with your financial planet, Mars, therefore you are provided with a great time for chasing money which is owed. Don't shillyshally or be too understanding of the excuses you are given, it's time to put your foot down in no uncertain fashion.

FRIDAY 10th   Mercury will be moving into fiery Sagittarius, so if you are trying to make any kind of travel arrangements, perhaps for the festive period, you could be in for a frustrating time. Double-check all of your facts, timetables, departures, otherwise you could get into a great deal of difficulty at a later date.

SATURDAY 11th   Mercury will be moving to the zenith point of your chart, suggesting that you have a couple of weeks for making minor adjustments to plans on the work front. Listen to the ideas of other people, too, they may not be as unique as your own but they may be a little bit more practical and the combination can lead to greater success.

SUNDAY 12th The time has come to speak your mind without worrying whether you are going to hurt somebody else's feelings. This won't come naturally, but once you begin you should find the going relatively easy and may even discover that others are grateful to you for having the courage to be open and honest.

MONDAY 13th Puzzles and dilemmas involving a combination of family and domestic issues have become a persistent worry, yet there has been no one answer that everyone concerned finds acceptable. Take heart, however, as solutions should soon arise. In the meantime, get out this evening and let of a little bit of steam, it will help chase away stress.

TUESDAY 14th In most cases, maintaining calm and serenity is something to be aimed for, but right now trying to promote a harmonious atmosphere could actually take the edge off certain developments. If other people are unsure about what to expect – from situations or you – then this may be the best way there is to keep them on their toes.

WEDNESDAY 15th There are some people who would say that being manipulative when dealing with difficult customers is dishonest, but most Pisceans understand that if delicate issues are tactfully presented, far more can be achieved than by being uncompromisingly blunt. Don't give up, even if the response is somewhat disappointing.

THURSDAY 16th You may be clear in your own mind about business or money matters, but don't imagine that others necessarily understand what is important to you. Remember this if it appears that certain people are trying to cut you out of discussions and you could nip misunderstandings in the bud.

FRIDAY 17th The Sun is in a beautiful aspect with Jupiter, so there is an optimistic and expansive feel about the day. This is a time for pushing ahead with everything that is important to you, whether personal, romantic or connected with work. Failure to utilize this day properly could be regretted at a later date.

SATURDAY 18th Don't let old frustrations overshadow this remarkable day when success in your efforts is very much a matter of who you are dealing with as well as good timing. If you are turned down by someone one day, you must simply pick yourself up and try all over again with someone else the next. Take heart.

SUNDAY 19th So much has been expected of you recently you are positively exhausted, but you need to soldier on for a while yet. Keep up your stamina by being sensible and make sure you keep a tight grip on cash and not only just your own. Those closest to you seem to be in an extravagant mood which could somehow rebound on you at a later date.

MONDAY 20th For some of you there's a possibility that you could fall on your feet where cash matters are concerned, whilst for others perhaps there is an exciting, unexpected present. However, for all, silly behaviour only exacerbates a difficult financial situation as well as displeasing other people, so control it.

TUESDAY 21st One friendship appears to be under some strain or stress. You don't understand quite how to find a compromise. You must keep trying because it is important to solve this particular thorny problem before the festive period arrives. You don't feel tremendously cooperative, though, so watch out for arguments.

WEDNESDAY 22nd Today is the day of the Full Moon and it occurs at the zenith point of your chart. If you are mixing business with pleasure, as is often the case at this time of the year, try not to push the boat out too far because you could fall over the edge, insult someone and possibly even lose your job – not very clever, I think you will agree.

THURSDAY 23rd Although you know in your hearts of hearts that being quiet is the only real sensible course at the moment, you still seem aggravated by the rather uppity or aloof attitude of somebody at work. Be prepared to stand up to them with charm and tact. In fact, it might be a good idea to give them a call and have a drink with them, perhaps around lunchtime or maybe this evening.

FRIDAY 24th The Sun is cosying up to your ruling

planet, Neptune, filling you with solar power, confidence and a great deal of warmth. Perhaps you've got that 'festive spirit' and if so, it would not be a good idea to take part in any late-night shopping, because your raid on the stores could very well be regretted at a later date.

SATURDAY 25th Although the atmosphere on the domestic front may be a little on the tense side, try to be more receptive to other people's way of thinking. This shouldn't be too difficult at this time because you are at your most adaptable and flexible, as well as affectionate. Minor changes can be made today, but nothing world-shattering please.

SUNDAY 26th You'll be at your most impressionable and other people could easily take advantage of you by being lavish with praise and flattery. You know what a sucker you can be when there is a silver tongue around to stroke that ego of yours. When will you learn, Pisces?

MONDAY 27th There seems to be a serious mood over family matters, but nothing too worrying. Perhaps just a family pow-wow or maybe a set of circumstances or problems that need some sorting through. As long as you don't avoid this, all should be well and conclusions will be reached.

TUESDAY 28th Mercury is in a beautiful aspect with Jupiter, so luckily for you those who are important in your life are in a humorous, happy-go-lucky mood which will lift the saddest of spirits. Not a good idea though to attend the sales, otherwise you'll commit grievous bodily harm to your bank account.

WEDNESDAY 29th   A foreigner or a visitor will play an influential role in your life today, or one that is very much to your advantage. Make plenty of time, too, for important personal and professional relationships. The more you invest in the way of time and energy in other people the more you will eventually receive in return.

THURSDAY 30th   Your imaginative powers are certainly at a peak right now and creative and artistic efforts are going to pay handsome dividends in the future. Any difficulties you feel you are faced with are purely imaginary, so try to put them in perspective.

FRIDAY 31st   Although you no doubt want to celebrate the New Year in a big way, just for once you are hoping that other people will be prepared to foot the bill. There's no logical reason why you're being so unfair, but hopefully you'll come to realize this and agree that the only way to travel is in harness where cash matters are concerned. Once you have sorted this matter out you can go ahead with all of your celebrations in the confident knowledge you've done the right thing.

Happy New Year!